# Family History 101

{ A Beginner's Guide To
Finding Your Ancestors }

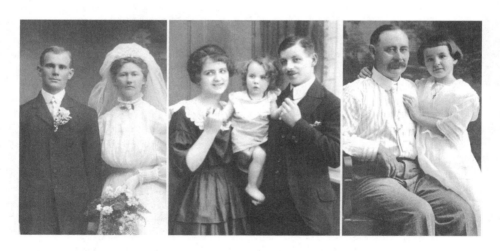

MARCIA D. YANNIZZE MELNYK

**FAMILY TREE BOOKS**
CINCINNATI, OH
www.familytreemagazine.com/store

Other fine Family Tree Books are available from your local bookstore or on our Web site at www.familytreemagazine.com/store.

09  08  07  06  05    5  4  3  2  1

**Library of Congress Cataloging-in-Publication Data**

Melnyk, Marcia Yannizze
  Family history 101 / Marcia D. Yannizze Melnyk.
    p.  cm.
  Includes bibliographical references and index.
  ISBN 1-55870-706-9 (pbk. : alk. paper)
  1. Genealogy. 2. United States—Genealogy—Handbooks, manuals, etc. I. Title: Family history one hundred one. II. Title.
CS16.M44  2005
929'.1'072073—dc22

2004058111
CIP

Editor: Sharon DeBartolo Carmack, CG
Associate editor: Erin Nevius
Production coordinator: Robin Richie
Production assistant: Logan Cummins
Interior designer: Sandy Conopeotis Kent
Cover design: Stanard Design Partners, Cincinnati, Ohio

I WOULD LIKE TO DEDICATE THIS BOOK
TO THE FOLLOWING PEOPLE:

❧ To my mother and "adopted father," Shirley Diana (Rogers) Pike
and Irving Pike, who have been two of my biggest fans. Their encouragement and support have been instrumental in my success.
They even keep copies of my books prominently displayed on the
bookshelf in their home. Irving's wonderful stories of "days gone
by" are always educational and enlightening, bringing to life the
lives of my ancestors in the New England area.

❧ To my friend and fellow genealogist, Marge (Panarello) DiSciullo,
whose ear I have bent on many occasions during the writing of this
book, I offer my heartfelt thanks. We have weathered some tough
times together, and like our ancestors we have triumphed, because
we supported each other, cried on each others' shoulders, and
didn't take ourselves too seriously! Hopefully she knows how much
her friendship means to me.

❧ Last but certainly not least, my husband Jim and daughter Diana,
who have made it through yet another manuscript process and lived
to tell about it! I will always be grateful for their support and pats
on the back when I needed them the most.

# Acknowledgments

While my name appears as the author on the cover of this book, there are additional individuals who deserve recognition. My fellow authors, lecturers, librarians, researchers, and friends require mention for their work, encouragement, education, and general patience during the process of compiling this manuscript. Any genealogist knows that we are continually learning about new records, strategies, and techniques. The network of researchers, specialists, helpful clerks, archivists, and librarians is one of the great joys of research. My heartfelt thanks go out to every single person who has helped me over the many years I have pursued my ancestors.

Special thanks must go to my editor and friend, Sharon DeBartolo Carmack, for allowing me to pick her brain, bounce ideas off of her, and to ask almost endless questions. She has taught me to reach inside and give the best I have while allowing me to be myself. Her patience and encouragement has meant the world to me. To my friend and fellow author, Maureen Taylor, I also extend my thanks for being there when I needed information, encouragement, and to lament my days with "writer's block." These two women have also taught me that extremely busy women can accomplish amazing things.

Thanks also go to my husband of thirty years, Jim, for all of his energy and encouragement. He spent many evenings alone while I plugged away in my office researching, writing, rewriting, and reworking chapters. The closer the manuscript came to completion the more time he spent alone, looking forward to our free time together. We both deserve it!

I also thank my wonderful ancestors, whose lives have enriched mine in so many ways. Their perseverance and accomplishments have taught me that nothing is impossible, and that we can overcome almost any obstacle if we keep our goals in sight, keep our faith, and support each other. I hope they are as proud of me as I am of them.

# Table of Contents

## About the Author

Marcia D. Yannizze Melnyk is a professional genealogist and lecturer. She is the author of *The Weekend Genealogist*, *The Genealogist's Handbook for New England Research*, 4th ed., *The Genealogist's Question & Answer Book*, and *The Ancestors and Descendants of Annabelle Whitehead and Anthony Pedro*. She created and taught the popular "Genealogy 101" course at the New England Historic Genealogical Society in Boston, Massachusetts, for nearly six years, and has lectured extensively throughout the United States and Canada. She is a member of the Association of Professional Genealogists, president and a founding member of the Italian Genealogical Society of America, and a former executive board member for the New England Regional Genealogical Conference (NERGC).

# Introduction

**F**amily history has become one of the most popular hobbies of our times. Millions of people, both in the United States and abroad, are searching for their ancestors and living relatives. The Internet has placed data and historical information at our fingertips. Information, both good and bad, can be sent around the world in seconds. Families that stretch around the globe can be in daily contact with each other with a mere click of the mouse. It is interesting that the study of history and our ancestors melds so seamlessly with the most modern technologies. We truly live in an exciting time to be family historians.

As family historians we have an obligation to research and accurately document those who went before us. We may begin with collections of research done by other family members or we may be the first in our family to document our ancestors, but regardless of where we start, we must be careful to make sure our family history is fact and not fiction. Documenting our research and checking any research done by others is important if we wish to leave a true story of our personal family history. True stories are far more compelling than any fiction.

I began my research with a need to obtain medical information for a physician. It started innocently enough by obtaining a few death records for aunts, uncles, and grandparents. Little did I know it would become a life-long quest—and a new career. One record led to another, more questions, more records, etc. If you are hooked on family history, you know the routine.

Over the years I have found many things that surprised me about my ancestors. Their difficult lives seemed so bleak at times that I wondered how they carried on day to day. My great-grandmother, Teresa Rebecca (Emery) Rogers, left a book of personal poetry chronicling her life over a period of more than sixty years. This intimate glimpse into her daily life— being orphaned as a small child, adopted, orphaned again, and seeing eleven of her fifteen children die—is the stuff novels are made of. But it's a million times more fascinating since someone actually lived through all this upheaval and pain, someone I am lucky enough to have as an ancestor. She may never have been rich or famous, but she is my role model and hero. She carried on and because of her, I am here.

The sheer mathematics of genealogy are staggering. Going back just to the tenth generation (about 250 years), every person has 1,024 eighth great-grandparents (512 couples in that one generation) who are directly responsible for your existence! If any one of those 1,024 individuals hadn't lived to have children, you wouldn't be here. This number doesn't even include all the aunts, uncles, cousins, etc.—just direct lineal ancestors! It's pretty amazing when you consider that each of these couples could then have four million or more descendents today.

So are you still ready to make the journey of a lifetime? You will have many ups and downs and frustrations during your search, but every brick wall you conquer, every ancestor you identify, and every story that you learn and record will make your life richer. You will come to understand history as you never expected to, and what's more amazing, how your family helped to form the history of so many lands. You will realize that you are a part of a much larger picture than your immediate family or town. We as a people are part of a global history. We include immigrants and emigrants, the conquerors and the conquered, royalty and slaves, and varied ethnic backgrounds. However, we're all human beings, with feelings, dreams, hardships, and triumphs—the fabric that comprises a life woven with so many others to form our past, present, and future. In the end we are so different and yet so much alike. Get ready for a wonderful journey!

**ONE**

# Why Genealogy?

R esearching and learning about our ancestors is one of the most popular hobbies of our time. It is pursued by young and old alike, those from every walk of life and every economic and ethnic group. Some call it genealogy while others, myself included, choose to refer to it as family history. Genealogy in its purest sense is the documenting of an individual's bloodline, stressing the *direct or lineal* ancestors as opposed to the *collateral lines*. Direct or lineal ancestors are best described as your bloodline. If any one of your lineal ancestors had not existed, neither would you. The lineal ancestors are your parents, grandparents, great-grandparents, etc. *Collateral lines* include those relatives from whom you do not descend. These are your aunts, uncles, cousins, siblings of your grandparents, etc.

## HELPFUL DEFINITIONS

**Genealogy:** "A record or table of the descent of the family group, or person from an ancestor or ancestors." (*The American Heritage Dictionary of the English Language*, by American Heritage Publishing Co., Inc., 1973)

**Collateral lines:** all relatives who are not directly (lineally) related; those families and persons related to the subject person through brothers or sisters of ancestors, or through marriage to such brothers and sisters." (*What Did They Mean by That?*, by Paul Drake, Baltimore, Md.: Heritage Books, Inc., 1994)

**Lineal:** in line of direct ascent or descent; relationship of parent to child through one or more generations. (*What Did They Mean by That?*, by Paul Drake, Heritage Books, Inc., 1994)

## GENEALOGY VS. FAMILY HISTORY

While some people will argue that what most researchers do is technically not genealogy but rather family history, the terms are often interchangeable in today's language. I prefer to use the term *family history*, as it more closely describes the type of research I do.

**\di'fin\ *vb***

**Definitions**

*Family history* **as a research exercise is much broader than traditional genealogy—it includes looking at the history of the time period, geographic location, and information about collateral relatives as well as the lineal ones.** Think about what is carved on a tombstone: Joseph A. Rogers, 1813–1853. His birth and death dates are a finite element in his life, but the dash between the dates has infinite research possibilities. Knowing what went on between 1813 and 1853 becomes *family history* in the truest sense of the term. What did Joseph do for a living? Whom did he marry? How many children did he have? What geographic locations did he live in? What caused his death at the young age of forty? What events were going on in the world that might have affected his life? What religion did he follow? What was his daily life like? Answers to all of these questions will reveal an individual interacting with other family and community members in many aspects of daily life. That is the *family history* that intrigues so many of us.

When we look for information about those relatives who came before us, we must keep in mind that our ancestors did not live in a vacuum. Extended families living in the same geographic areas were the norm prior to the mid-twentieth century. Family meant more than just parents and children—it included cousins (first, second, third, etc.), aunts, uncles, nieces, and nephews, as well as relatives by marriage. The *family* that is often referred to was also the support system for each individual family member. The more recent generations of families have stepsiblings, stepparents, etc., to add to the mix. Therefore, family encompasses a much wider group of people than just your direct ancestors. This makes our research far-reaching and more widely focused than previous generations of genealogists and family historians. Some refer to this type of research as *cluster genealogy*. We must look at not only our direct relatives by blood and marriage, but at all of the individuals that interact with our family members. We must consider all of these individuals *extended family*.

## WHAT MOTIVATES US?

Why do we research our ancestors? The reasons are almost as varied as the people who perform the research. Some search for medical reasons, others for the sheer curiosity of it. An interest in history also plays into the puzzle, as world events shaped generations of lives both here and abroad. Remember that our ancestors did not live in isolation any more than we do today. Work, sports, world events, tragedies, and celebrations were just as much a part of their lives as they are ours and affected them just as they do us. Dreams and goals were rethought, changed, and adjusted according to the events happening in their lives and the world they lived in. Different time periods meant different expectations and opportunities for any single individual. Social and economic conditions, as well as the custom of the time, determined what occupations were available for men and women. We tend to forget that there were certain jobs that you were almost born into, such as farming, and that few opportunities presented themselves that allowed you to change your status in life.

Understanding how your ancestors lived and what restrictions they lived under tends to make most researchers in the twenty-first century appreciate the freedoms we have today. Women as well as men have many more opportunities to pursue, occupations to try, and freedoms that were unimaginable to even our grandparents' generation.

I am a believer in the hypothesis that we as researchers are selected by our ancestors to carry on the family research and pass the information on to future generations. Rarely are two individuals in the same family interested in genealogy. In all the years I have been teaching, I can only recall one or two instances where two siblings worked together on the research. While other relatives may be interested in the information, there is most often only one person in each family actually doing the work.

When you first began researching you may have had no intention of making it a lifelong project, but family history has a way of pulling you in. With each new relative you find the same questions must be answered. Every answer leads to more questions. **It's never-ending for most people.** Many spend their entire lives researching, using every spare minute to trace their elusive ancestors. Relatives may voice the opinion that we are nuts. "Why are you interested in dead people?," is a question many of you have probably heard. I can't think of a set answer to it other than I would like to be remembered after I am gone, and I have a need to honor those who went before me by telling their story.

History was not one of my favorite subjects in school, but learning about it in the context of my family's history and knowing of the ancestors who took part in these events makes the entire subject come to life. Learning

Warning

and recording only the names and dates made boring history lessons, and if that's all you explore, they'll make a boring family history as well. You must understand that your ancestors lived within the context of time and history. Whether they came to the United States with the Pilgrims or in one of the many waves of immigration from foreign countries, they have a history that needs to be told. Politics, religious freedom, persecution, starvation, job opportunities, and so many other reasons led many of our ancestors to flee their native country and settle in an unknown land. Their struggles to survive, provide for their families, and for some, to actually prosper are the tales that make up our family history.

When I look back over my lifetime I realize that I was probably destined to be the family historian. Long before my research began, I named my daughters after grandparents that I had never personally known. I don't know why this small act was so important to me over twenty years ago, but I remember feeling as though I had to pass their names along to another generation. The most amazing thing is that my oldest daughter, Diana, looks so much like her namesake it's scary!

I have a portrait of my grandmother, Diana Belle Rounds, that I cherish, taken when she was about eighteen years old (see Figure 1-1 on page 7). One afternoon my daughter Diana, then sixteen, came downstairs after taking a shower. She had her long golden brown hair twisted on top of her head in a little bun. As she walked by the picture of my grandmother, the similarities jumped out at me. My grandmother's portrait was taken about 1910 and her hair was atop her head in a little bun. The shape and structure of their faces were the same. Not having seen my daughter with her hair up very often, I hadn't noticed the similarities in their looks. It is amazing that, of all the ancestors she could have looked like, it was her namesake's face that she bore.

Over the last fifteen plus years of teaching and consultations, I have met many individuals and heard many stories regarding the reasons for their search. Some of the reasons I have heard include adoptions, separated families (through divorce or death), family skeletons or heroes, medical information, to join a lineage society, a photograph, family Bibles or papers, etc. The one theme that seems to recur is the need to know about those who went before us. Perhaps it is our need to understand ourselves and how we fit into the broader scope of the world that intrigues us. Maybe we need to understand something about ourselves—who we look like, our personalities and habits. **Many adopted individuals have expressed the need**

Important

**Figure 1-1**
Oval portrait of Diana Belle
(Rounds) Rogers.

**to know where they come from.** I remember one young man telling me, after finding his birth mother, that he saw a picture of his biological grandfather and finally knew who he looked like. While this need may be stronger in adoptees than in others, the curiosity is still evident in most researchers.

Throughout my research I've learned about my ancestors' lives, families, and in some cases, their personalities. Some stories are tragic, others downright humorous. All of the stories were more interesting than I could ever have imagined. How my ancestors helped create the history of not only this nation but so many others around the world made me realize how much one individual in any society can change history simply by existing!

My great-grandmother, Teresa Rebecca (Emery) Rogers, left a handwritten book of poetry about her life and family. The poems, written over a sixty-year time period, chronicled the family in a very touching way. Teresa and her husband, Hoxey Rogers, had fifteen children, only four of whom survived to adulthood. Hoxey Rogers witnessed the burial of thirteen of his children in his lifetime of eighty-seven years. He and Teresa lost four children in one month (three in the same week), and yet they managed to go on. To read the thoughts, joys, and pains of my great-grandmother was an incredible thing. I often think of her and wonder if I could be as

**Figure 1-2**
Hoxey and Teresa (Emery)
Rogers.

strong as she was during such trying times. She was never famous or wealthy, yet she is and always will be my hero (see Figure 1-2 above).

## OFF ON A JOURNEY

Whatever the impetus, you are now engaged in a journey of knowledge about not only your ancestors, but about yourself. What makes you the unique person that you are? What characteristics of your ancestors, both physical and personal, do you possess? Many good as well as bad traits are passed down for generations. Learning about both the negatives and the positives will give you incredible insight into your personality and those of your relatives. Understanding the time period in which they lived and what events, both local and worldwide, affected their lives will give you better insight into their dreams, goals, happiness, and heartaches.

If we think back to September 11, 2001, we could all write an essay about how we felt and how those tragic events changed our lives. The same holds true for those who lived through the two world wars, the attack on Pearl Harbor, the Civil War, the assassination of President Kennedy, and so many other events. Decisions made by our ancestors to leave a foreign land for America or to go westward to the frontier were often made as a solution to some problem, either personal or economic. Others simply suffered from wanderlust or had a need to outrun some legal authority.

In many cases, understanding the family situations of previous generations can unravel family mysteries and help us accept people for who they are. Walk a mile in their moccasins, and you will get a better picture of why they are who they are.

## Family Stories and Healing

Here's an example: My father was born into a melded family consisting of a father, Bruno, and a mother, Amelia, who had both been previously married. The eight children born of these earlier marriages were all part of the family. Bruno and Amelia had three children of their own, creating an extended family of eleven children and their collective parents. Before I began my research no one in the family could tell me how we were all related.

My father had two half-brothers (sons from Amelia's first marriage), David and Patrick. Patrick died when I was just a small child and I never knew him personally. David, on the other hand, had come in and out of our lives at different times, mostly at family gatherings. I always found it hard to believe that he was even related to my father, let alone his brother. The two men were as opposite as any two men can be. Dave was a very successful businessman who owned his own company. He was what my father referred to as a "workaholic" and did not spend a lot of time with his family. He did, however, idolize his mother, Amelia.

My father was an automobile mechanic who owned his own service stations and raised five children of his own. He was a gentle but strict man who was always there for his children. While he worked long hours at times, he was always home for dinner and important events. We took a two-week family vacation every summer. I have many happy memories of my childhood and the fun we all had.

When my father was diagnosed with inoperable cancer, his family became even more important to him. We all gathered around, helped whenever we could, and simply enjoyed the time we had left by listening to stories of his childhood. His siblings visited often, with the exception of Dave. My father often asked for Dave and wanted to see him. Amelia passed away in March 1973, just six months before my father, and the last time we had seen Dave was at her funeral. I tried calling him on numerous occasions to let him know that Dad wanted to see him. It seemed that Dave always had an excuse why he couldn't come. It became more apparent that my Dad was nearing the end of his struggle and my uncle had still not visited. In spite of my almost daily calls to him, he never came. My father passed away without ever seeing his brother again, and I had a hard time understanding how Dave could do this to his only living brother.

Many years passed and I pushed Dave out of my mind, still angry with him for not granting my father his dying wish. Then, in 1988, nearly fifteen years after my father's death, I signed up for a genealogy course at the local library. There were only ten students enrolled and one of them was Dave's daughter! We struck up a conversation, and I learned that Dave had been diagnosed with cancer the previous year. It seemed an ironic twist of fate that his daughter and I should meet again at this time.

Since we were learning about doing oral histories, I decided to visit Dave and see if I could shed any light on his actions. I also wanted to hear stories of his childhood and perhaps even about my father. After I visited with him several times at his daughter's house, he was put into a nursing home not far from my home. I took the opportunity to visit him often. For me these visits were enjoyable and very informative. Sometimes I would pick up my aunt, his sister, and we would go together. Dave often complained to us that his son and daughter rarely visited—they were always too busy.

Dave told us about his unhappy childhood. Apparently, when Amelia married Bruno in 1911 he refused to allow her two sons, David and Patrick, to live with them, as they were another man's children. At first I thought this was a terrible thing to do and that my grandmother would never have stood for it. But history led me to reconsider. A single mother really had no choice in 1911. Amelia raised Bruno's children and his illegitimate daughter, but was not allowed to raise her own sons. They were sent to live at Amelia's parents' home a few blocks away from their mother and could only visit when Bruno was not at home.

The story continued to unfold over the next few visits. Dave told us that he and Patrick would walk home from school past their mother's house. My father, Joe, would signal them from the upper floor windows as to whether they could come in or not. If Bruno was in the house they walked on past and continued to their grandparents. Dave often referred to himself as "the poor little orphan," and commented that it was my father who told him he couldn't come in.

My aunt reminded Dave that he was lucky to live with his grandparents since my father, Joe, was often beaten by Bruno. Joe would actually step in front of his sisters and take a beating to protect them from Bruno's wrath. Dave said that he would willingly have taken a beating to live with his mother. It finally dawned on me that Dave had blamed my father all of these years for his unhappy childhood. As a small boy he could not be angry at or hate his mother for allowing the situation to continue, so he blamed the only other person he could—my father.

This revelation was a wonderful healing for me and for the rest of the family. Dave, although in his eighties, was still that hurt little boy. His drive to prove he was better than my father was a lifelong mission that even he did not understand. Forgiveness is a lot easier when you have heard both sides of the story.

I often wonder how many other stories have died with their holder, never to be revealed. When an individual dies, they take an entire library of information and stories with them. Our goal as family historians is to document as much as we can to preserve it for our descendants and future family historians.

## DETERMINING YOUR RESEARCH GOALS

Have you given some thought as to what you are hoping to gain in the pursuit of your family history? Whatever the impetus is to research, you need a plan before you proceed.

**Notes**

**The questions you should now ask yourself are:**

- What are my goals?
- What will I eventually do with all of the information I accumulate?
- How will I share my information with other family members or researchers?
- Do I want to trace just the male or surname lines or the maternal lines as well?
- What information about their lives do I want to find?
- How will I compile that information?

All of these questions will help you form a strategy and lay the groundwork for your future research.

Once you have answered these questions, you are ready to begin. Always begin with yourself and work backward through time, from the known to the unknown. Proving each generation one at a time will save you many hours of research in the future. If you have an adoptee for an ancestor, you will need to decide whether to trace the biological or adoptive lines. Many researchers will eventually do both, since personality characteristics can be acquired through both lines. Nature or nurture is still debated in many scientific circles. While I may never know where my adopted great-grandmother, Teresa, got her beautiful blue eyes, I do know that her adoptive family instilled in her the importance of education and her lifelong love of books and knowledge. Teresa's adoptive mother was an ancestor of Anne Bradstreet, one of the first female poets in the United States.

With today's wonderful technology and the wealth of genealogical programs for sale, there are almost as many ways to keep track of your information as there are researchers. You might use computer programs to record your data or adhere to the tried and true method of paper charts and records. Use the technique that fits your style. No computer program or paper chart can get or keep you organized if you do not use it. Understanding your personal style of management and incorporating a filing system that fits that style is a major key to your success. (More in-depth information on the subject of organization will be discussed in chapter three.)

Have you determined your goals and decided how best to achieve them? Then let's get started!

**TWO**

# Where Do I Begin?

## FIRST THINGS FIRST

The best way to begin is by writing down what you already know (or think you know). This includes personal information regarding your birth, marriage, children, etc. List the same information for your parents and siblings. Remember to list both the dates and the locations where these events took place. See how far back you can go with names and approximate dates. Keep in mind that all of these details must eventually be proven—*they cannot be taken as fact until you have documented verification*. You may encounter many surprises as you progress with your research. This can make the process interesting. No one in my family knew that my great-grandmother was adopted until I uncovered it. You may find any number of "skeletons" in your family history closet. Remember to accept the bad with the good—being judgmental and avoiding such facts can cause inaccurate information to be passed along. Many relatives never speak of these skeletons, and as a result, many of the interesting individuals in our family never come to light. **It is important to remember that all of your ancestors were human beings with faults and frailties just like ours.** While they may have made mistakes in their lives, it is how they overcame their problems and continued to persevere that makes them come alive! Good or bad, they are our ancestors. Who is to say that we would not have made some of the same decisions and mistakes if we were in their time and place?

Most school- and college-aged students find history to be a boring subject. The people included in the history books seem larger-than-life and are held in such high regard that students find it difficult to relate to them as individuals. Think of George Washington and how he is described in

Important

most of the history books. There is little that makes him seem human. He's often portrayed as a hero able to accomplish anything.

While reading and doing some research on the Revolutionary War, I met a man who specialized in this era of America's history. He told me several stories about Washington that made me realize he was also a shrewd businessman for his time. The man told me that before and during the Revolutionary War, Washington kept most of his money in the Bank of England rather than in banks in his adopted land. After the war was won, he wrote to England to obtain his fortune. With the exception of the fact that the Bank of England refused to address him as General Washington, they sent him his funds. Others weren't so fortunate. Many, including my fourth great-grandfather, lost most of what they had when independence from England was gained and English currency was no longer valid.

Another eye-opening revelation occurred when I attended a lecture on the Tories (those loyal to England in the Revolutionary War). I heard stories of the punishments dealt to those who remained loyal to the crown by those wishing to break away from English rule. I don't recall seeing any of those stories in the history books of years ago. Many lost not only their land and homes, but their families as well. Homes were burned to the ground, people were tarred and feathered, and many fled to Canada to save their lives. All they'd accumulated in their lives was lost—taken from them simply because they had different loyalties than the majority.

Always keep in mind that history books are written from the point of view of the winner and may only include the parts they wish to convey. Things they are not proud of may be omitted to make themselves look better. The same is true for any family stories you might hear or know about. Key facts or individuals may be omitted or "rearranged" to cover up embarrassing facts. Always keep an open mind and gather all the information in order to prove or disprove what you've heard.

## FAMILY PAPERS AND ORAL HISTORY

That said, let's move on to family papers and oral history. Some families have boxes of family papers, while others seem to have none. When you begin asking relatives for information, be sure to ask about any family papers that might exist—whether they think they are of interest to you or not. Many of these papers may not interest you early in your research, but later, when you know a lot more about the family unit, they might hold the clue you need to solve a mystery. But will you know where these papers are when you need them? Perhaps the person owning all the family pictures and papers has since died, and the box of "stuff" has been tossed or passed on to another relative.

Photocopies are cheap insurance against such a loss. We now have digital scanners and photocopiers available to us. **Make duplicates of the pictures or documents by scanning them onto a computer, or have negatives made from the original photos.** When you scan great-grandma's marriage record you will have an accurate copy with all of the aged color of the original document. You can also make as many copies as you wish without handling the original more than necessary. You can share copies to be framed and displayed without worrying about damaging or losing the original.

Tip

## SUGGESTED READING

*Caring for Family Treasures: Heritage Preservation*, by Jane S. Long & Richard W. Long (Abrams Publishers, 2000)

*Living Legacies: How to Write, Illustrate and Share Your Life Stories*, by Duane Elgin and Coleen LeDrew (Conari Press, 2001)

*Preserving Your Family Photographs*, by Maureen A. Taylor (Cincinnati: Betterway Books, 2001)

*Uncovering Your Ancestry through Family Photographs*, by Maureen A. Taylor (Cincinnati: Betterway Books, 2000)

*Writing Family Histories and Memoirs*, by Kirk Polking (Cincinnati: Betterway Books, 1995)

For More Info

To learn more about preserving and recording your family history, see *Organizing & Preserving Your Heirloom Documents*, by Katherine Scott Sturdevant (Cincinnati: Betterway Books, 2002), *Scrapbooking Your Family History*, by Maureen A. Taylor (Cincinnati: Betterway Books, 2003), and *You Can Write Your Family History*, by Sharon DeBartolo Carmack (Cincinnati: Betterway Books, 2003).

I've been working on a project for quite some time that has provided me with many wonderful pictures of my ancestors that I never knew existed. I began by scanning all of the old photos I had of my parents, grandparents, etc. After creating digital files of the images, I sent copies to my cousins who shared the same ancestors. I soon received copies of additional photographs that they had in their collections, greatly widening the scope of my photographic history. Since I had the ability to do the scanning, others loaned me whole collections of photos to scan into the ever-growing digital database.

I then met with the curator of the Historical Society in Troy, New Hampshire, where my mother grew up. They have a large collection of photos from schools, local businesses, etc. that has been donated over the years by residents or their descendants. After scanning and digitizing their entire

---

**HOME DOCUMENTS**

- BOOKS—Bibles, diaries, journals, yearbooks, account books, baby books, scrapbooks, and biographies.

- CERTIFICATES—birth, christening, baptismal, confirmation, ordination, graduation, marriage, divorce, and death.

- NEWSPAPERS—clippings from births, christenings, announcements, engagements, marriages, divorces, awards, deaths, obituaries, memorials, property transfers, etc.

- LAND & ESTATE RECORDS—deeds, mortgages, leases, wills, trust documents, tax records.

- MILITARY RECORDS—enlistment or induction notices, rosters, muster rolls, discharges, citations, pension records, etc.

- MISC. RECORDS—letters, pictures, naturalization, passports, school/university records, lodge, club and fraternity, business and insurance records, receipts and accounts.

collection, I indexed all of the names listed on the back of the photographs. After burning (or recording) the photos on CD-ROM disks (I made four sets of copies), I returned the originals to the historical society. Two members of the society have a set of disks, and another remains at the historical society along with the original photos. I also kept a set of my own. The collection can now be replaced should any disaster destroy the originals. The index also enables the society to easily check the collection when they receive an inquiry from a researcher. In return, I found more than forty photographs of family members within the collection.

I have only begun to tap into all of the possible papers and photos held by cousins, aunts, uncles, or other collateral family. Thus far I have borrowed, scanned, digitized, and burned to CD-ROM only two collections. I know that there will be surprises as I make my way through the other eighteen of my first cousins, let alone all my other relatives. In addition to photographs, there are also numerous documents to look for among home papers, records, or correspondence.

## THE ORAL HISTORY INTERVIEW

Once you have found, copied, and reviewed all of the family papers, I bet you'll have some questions regarding these documents. Now is a good time to interview your relatives.

Recording an oral history can be a very special way to preserve the thoughts, ideas, and memories of another time and place. It is also a method of holding on to your ancestors, to hear their voices and see their unique expressions and mannerisms many years from now. We'd all like to avoid the realization that our loved ones will not always be with us, but we have the opportunity to do what our parents and grandparents couldn't. The invention of audio and video recorders allows us to preserve for our children and future generations that which made our ancestors the special individuals they were. We can also record and save our own memories in the same way.

---

**THINGS TO REMEMBER ABOUT "FAMILY STORIES"**

- There is usually a grain of truth in the story somewhere.

- Not all stories are based on fact.

- Not all family stories are positive.

- Family stories usually have no documentation.

Depending on the timeframe of the story, it has been passed on, added to, and modified many times over the generations.

---

## Steps to Take for a Successful Oral History Interview

1. Determine who your subject will be. This could be an older family member, an older member of the community in which your deceased ancestor lived, people who lived in the same time period, or someone of the same ethnic group to which your ancestor belonged.

2. Discuss the possibility of interviewing your subject in advance of doing the actual interview. Let the subject know that they have the final say in what goes into the written or audio version before it is completed or shared with others.

3. Determine a time and location for the interview. This should be a time when you can meet with the subject one-on-one for an hour or more. Consider the age and health of your subject when determining how long to make the session. Multiple sessions are always a good idea. Once the memory retrieval process has begun your subject will remember many things both during and after the initial session.

4. Compile a notebook of records and papers pertinent to the subject

**Tip**

**HELPFUL HINT**

To determine what world or local events happened during any given period of time, visit your local library and browse through newspapers from the years you are researching.

and your family. Include any papers that show the subject in a census record, naturalization papers, passenger lists, etc. I always leave this notebook as a gift for the person I interview. Look for books pertaining to the geographic area the subject lived in during the period of their lives you are interested in (the earlier the better).

5. Determine what local or world events took place during their lifetime. Newspapers are a wonderful way to find out what was going on in the town, state, or world in any given time period. You will want to ask questions about how these events shaped their lives and futures.

**Warning**

6. Make a list of questions to ask the individual. **Avoid "yes" or "no" questions—open-ended questions will get your subject talking and help jog their memory.** Include some fact-based questions like "When and where were you born?" or "How many brothers and sisters did your grandfather have?" Begin with fact-based questions and gradually progress into personal recollections as your subject becomes more comfortable with the process. Avoid the temptation to interrupt your subject's train of thought. Be silent while the subject reflects on the memory they are relaying. Never correct your subject or indicate that you think they are wrong—even if you have facts to back it up! Be careful and compassionate when dealing with sensitive subjects such as children born out of wedlock, criminal activities within the family, deaths, etc. Be nonjudgmental!

7. If you want to tape, whether video or audio, be sure to obtain permission from the subject during your initial contact when setting up the interview. Many times they are reluctant to let themselves be taped. This can stem from a fear of saying something they will regret revealing or just a dislike of having their picture taken. Remember to let them know that they can delete any comment or subject from the finished tape. If you do tape the interview, make sure that the camera or recorder is off to the side and not in obvious view of your subject.

8. Make sure you have a comfortable, quiet, and private place to conduct the interview—outside distractions will hinder it. Obtain the longest tapes possible to avoid changing tapes or stopping the subject to turn tapes over. Avoid all reminders that they're being recorded once the interview begins. If you have one-hour tapes, prepare to take a short break after forty-five or fifty minutes of interviewing. This will give your subject time to think, and you will have time to change tapes discretely. Depending on the age and health of your subject, one-hour sessions may be best.

9. Ask the subject to write down things that come to mind after the session and save them for a future interview. You can also leave a list of questions for them to answer after the session (only if writing is not difficult for them). Once you begin the memory retrieval process, you'll be amazed at how much people remember. Make sure to do a follow-up with your subject a week or so after the interview. This is when you can ask about any subsequent memories that may have surfaced. Keep the dialogue open between you and the subject.

10. If time allows, look for one of the many books available in book and gift stores to give to your subject, either before or at the time of the interview. These books are sometimes called *Grandparents' Books, To My Daughter or Son*, etc. They have questions, comments, and space for people to write their memories of specific events and people in their lives.

11. Always thank your subject and ask if you may contact them with any questions that might come up, for clarification of something they said or just to tell them thank you. Follow through on your commitment to erase anything they wish to delete from the taped interview and then never repeat it to anyone.

12. If there is sensitive information contained in the interview, ask the subject what they wish you to do with it. I have had several subjects who said "Don't let anyone know as long as I am alive." Sometimes it's a relief to be able to release these secrets to another person after keeping them inside for many years.

The following list should get you started, but don't limit yourself to these questions.

### Family Facts
1. How old are you now? When and where were you born?
2. How many brothers and sisters are there in your family? What was their order of birth?
3. What is your first memory as a child? Why do you think that memory is so vivid?
4. What type of child were you (happy, shy, outgoing, etc.)?

### Parents
1. Who were your parents?
2. Where was your mother born? When?

3. What was your mother's maiden name? What were her parents' names?

4. What was her given name? Did she have a nickname? What was it?

5. Did she have brothers and sisters? How many? What were their names?

6. Where was your father born? When?

7. What were his parents' names?

8. Did he have brothers and sisters? How many? What were their names?

9. Do you know who the first person was in your family to come to the United States? What country did he/she emigrate from? When? Did they say why they emigrated?

10. Do you know when or how your parents met?

11. Did they ever talk about their courtship or the early days of their marriage?

12. Where did they live? Did they move around much? Why (e.g. work, military, etc.)?

13. What do you recall about the house that you grew up in?

14. What did it look like? Were there many other families on the street? What were their names?

15. Were there any special places in the neighborhood (e.g. corner store, playground, etc.)?

16. Did your mother work outside the home? Doing what? If she didn't work outside the home, what kinds of things did she do?

17. Did she like to cook? Was she a good cook? What were your favorite foods that she made? Why?

18. Did she ever let you help with the chores? Which ones did you particularly like to help with? Why? Which ones did you dislike to do? Why?

19. What family traditions do you remember from your childhood? Have they continued on in your generation?

**Grandparents**

1. What were their names? Where were they from? Where were they born?

2. Do you remember them? What special names did you call them? Did they have nicknames or pet names for you or your siblings? How did these names come to be?

3. Do you recall what they looked like (tall, short, thin, heavy, bald, bearded, etc.)? What type of personality did they have?

4. What were their occupations, education, and special skills?

5. Does anything in particular stand out about them (sense of humor, etc.)?

6. Do you have any especially vivid memories of time you spent with them?

7. Do you know how or when they died? Do you know where they are buried?

8. Did they have any special habits or traditions that continue in your family today?

9. Are there any family heirlooms or property that have been handed down from your grandparents to the current generation? What? To whom did it first belong? Did it hold some special meaning or significance in their lives? To whom will it be passed on? Is there a special significance to this choice (e.g. first son, youngest daughter, etc.)?

**Personal Opinions and Outlook**

1. What everyday conveniences do we have today that were not available when you were a child/young adult/newlywed?

2. What were the major issues and worries that faced you then? How were they different than today's problems?

3. What world events affected your life the most and why?

4. Were you as aware of the events in the world as we are today?

5. What were your major concerns for the future?

6. What were your dreams or expectations for the future? Which came to pass? Which did not?

7. What events in your life, if any, caused you to change your expectations or goals? Were the changes for the better or do you have regrets?

8. Do you think it was easier then or now to reach the goals we set for ourselves? Why?

9. If you could go back in time, knowing what you know now, what, if anything would you change? Why?

10. What was the most rewarding time or event in your life? Why?

11. What single piece of advice would you like to give me?

There are also many fun things to inquire about—their teen years, how they met their spouse, where they went while dating, and things their children did while growing up. These questions are important when a person interviews their grandparents. They have recollections of the interviewer's parents as children as well as adults. Grandchildren love to hear stories about their parents as children. Hearing about someone you know in an entirely different role can be enlightening as well as humorous.

**Fun Questions to Add to the Interview**

1. What were some of the fads or styles among young people when you were a teenager?
2. What were some of the slang expressions used?
3. How did the girls and boys wear their hair?
4. What were the fads or trends that your parents did not like or approve of?
5. Who were your best friends?
6. What was your first car? What do you remember about it?
7. What was your first job? How long did you work there?

Always remember to thank your subject when you are through, and always try to make it an enjoyable time together. If need be, you can schedule another interview date at this time.

## Important Things to Remember

**Important**

In addition to interviewing relatives and others who have information about your relatives, remember that you also have memories that will be important to future generations of genealogists and historians. **Writing down or taping your own memories is just as important as recording others.** After completing this list with your interview subject, think about the questions as they pertain to you. Remember that your grandchildren or great-grandchildren might be interested in the same things about your life in the future.

Learning about your ancestor as a person is much more interesting than the names and dates you pull from official records. What was her daily life like? How did world events direct her life? What were her dreams and aspirations for the future? What people or events redirected these goals?

Now write down *your* answers to the same questions as if a descendant was interviewing you. You can always go back and rewrite them if other stories pop into your mind. You will be amazed at how many memories you have. Don't worry about perfect grammar or punctuation. Would you criticize these things if you suddenly came across such writings for your great-grandparents? Just reading their words and thoughts would be more important than the spelling or grammar.

Try writing down specific memories that you think of from time to time. Do you have memories of your grandparents? Great-grandparents? Even memories of your children will be important to their descendants in the future. Try to include how you felt about certain events, people, and your life. The sad stories can be as enlightening as the sweet. You may believe that your life is boring or uninteresting, but remember that your memories will become as valuable to your descendants as the memories of your ancestors are to you!

Let this project be the foundation for a wonderful legacy for your grandchildren. Most of all, enjoy the adventure!

## SOCIAL HISTORIES AND NEWSPAPERS

Another way to understand the lives of previous generations, especially those who are no longer with us (or if you have no one to interview about them), is through social history and newspapers. An interesting and valuable book is *Bringing Your Family History to Life Through Social History* by Katherine Scott Sturdevant (Cincinnati, Ohio: Betterway Books, 2000). Learning as much as possible about their specific time and place will help you understand the events and lifestyles that had an influence on your ancestors.

**Social histories can also provide information about:**

- certain immigrant groups and their origins in the old country.
- local businesses that can provide you with clues to the reasons your ancestors settled where they did, and perhaps the occupation they chose. Was there a large factory in the area? Coal mines? What industries were prevalent?
- wars or military conflicts that occurred in the location where your ancestors lived.
- the socioeconomics of the geographic area.

Reminder

Social histories are a wonderful window into the past, and when used in conjunction with newspapers from the time period, they can provide you with a better understanding of the era your ancestors lived in. Newspapers can also provide wonderful information about the local climate and social lives of individuals.

When looking at old newspapers I enjoy looking at the classified ads, particularly those listing housing prices or rental costs. Ads from local stores can create a fun dimension to your recorded family history. We might laugh at some of these ads today, but they are a sign of the times and give us a peek at another time and place. Who's to say that the newspaper ads of today won't be comical one hundred years from now?

Many newspapers also had social columns. These columns often mention groups of people engaged in clubs, organizations, or even school events. Many churches also had gatherings that might be noted in the local paper. In addition, the local news may shed some light on family events that occurred. Newspapers are not just for obituaries and marriage notices! Watch for articles published in the time periods around specific family events such as graduations, job advancements, anniversaries (especially twenty-fifth and fiftieth), retirements, first communions, Bar Mitzvahs, or other religious milestones. The possibilities are endless once you get started. Remember—the more interesting you make the family history, the more likely it is that others will read it. Except to the family genealogist, lists of names and dates are not very interesting. Punch it up with social history and stories or ads from the local newspapers.

Now that you have accumulated the information from home sources and interviews, you will need to begin recording and proving all of that information. Remember that a good foundation is necessary to build a solid family history!

**THREE**

# Recording Data

 One of the most important components of laying a solid founda-tion for your family history is recording your research with stan-dard forms. The basic forms you'll need to start are:

- pedigree charts
- family group sheets
- research log sheets
- blank records forms to record data found

Begin by familiarizing yourself with these forms. Transfer all your proven data to them before you start any new research. **By using standard forms you'll have as concise a record as possible.** Librarians and other re-searchers will be able to tell at a glance where you are in your research and what to help you with first.

Hand-drawn charts confuse everyone but the person who drew them. With all of the effort and time you'll be expending on research, you should always record the data in a businesslike manner. Loose papers, notes, hand-drawn charts, etc. can look messy and unimportant to others. By keeping the records neatly on standard forms in an orderly fashion, you ensure that those papers likely will not be tossed when you are gone. You spent a lot of time researching and preparing these records—make them look as important as they are! You can download these forms for free from the Family Tree Magazine Web site <www.familytreemagazine.com/forms/download.html>.

Let's start with the *pedigree chart*. This chart records only your lineal ancestors. (See Figure 3-1 on page 28.) There are many different styles,

Tip

and you will find one that best suits your needs after some trial and error. However, all styles of pedigree charts are basically generic. They should have six lines of information for each person. This means that there should be a place to record not only the date of a life event (birth, marriage, or death) but also the location where the event took place. All pedigree charts show the same information and the format is basically the same.

The *family group sheet* is the next standard form you must acquaint yourself with. It's a listing of just one couple and all their biological children (see Figure 3-2 on page 29). If either of the parents has children by a different spouse, they should have a separate sheet for that family group. Not everyone agrees on whether adopted children should be included on these sheets along with biological children, but if you do include them, be sure to record the adoption facts as well as the birth, marriage, and death dates and locations. Since every state in the U.S. creates a new birth certificate at the time of the adoption (listing the adoptive parents as the biological ones), your notations might be the only clue to this fact. Since medical history can be important, it may become crucial to know that a person is not a blood relative.

## RECORDING DATA ON CHARTS

- *All surnames (last names) should be written in capital letters.* It is important to clearly indicate which name is the surname and which is the given name on your genealogical charts. Particularly with immigrant names, this can be confusing. You can record with either the surname or given name first, but capitalization clarifies the issue:

  EXAMPLE: James Dexter GEORGE

- *If the middle name is known, spell it out completely. Don't use just an initial.* Many individuals used their middle name rather than their given name. Sometimes it was done to distinguish between two people with the same name, or perhaps they just didn't like their given name. In some cultures, children are given a saint's name as their first name and then another name by which they are addressed. Maria Teresa SCALI was called Teresa, and her sister, Maria Assunta SCALI, was called Assunta.

  EXAMPLE: Marcia D. YANNIZZE should be Marcia Diane YANNIZZE.

- *If a person was known by a nickname, put that name in quotation marks and always record it.* Since many people were known throughout their lives by nicknames, there may be records listed under that name. My grandfather, Seneca Baker ROGERS, was always known as Joe ROGERS. Many people never knew that his given name was Seneca. People sometimes recorded him as Joseph ROGERS since they assumed that Joe was short for Joseph. I've found him recorded as Joseph B. ROGERS, Joe S. ROGERS, and many other combinations.

  EXAMPLE: Seneca Baker "Joe" ROGERS

- *Females should always be listed using their maiden surnames, not married names.* When listing a female on pedigree charts, you should be careful to record all the surnames she had during her lifetime, in the order in which she acquired them.

  EXAMPLE: Mrs. Diana Belle ROGERS was born Diana Belle ROUNDS and should only be recorded as Diana Belle ROUNDS.

  If Diana Belle ROUNDS married John SMITH as her second husband you would record her as Diana (ROUNDS) (ROGERS) SMITH, being sure to always list her maiden name first and her subsequent married names in the order in which she acquired them.

  If you know a woman's married surnames but not her maiden name, you should record her as Diana (—?—) (ROGERS) SMITH, indicating that you know another surname exists but it's currently unknown to you.

- *Dates should be recorded using the following format: 9 FEB 1951.* Using the common date format in the United States of 2/9/51 can and will be misinterpreted by some people. Is February 9 or September 2 being recorded? In Europe, February 9, 1951, would be written 9/2/51, since they list the dates in day, month, and year order. Is the year 1851 or 1951? When the record is viewed out of context the year needs to be clearly written. Knowing which century is crucial! By using the 9 FEB 1951 format, there is no chance for misinterpretation.

  EXAMPLE: 21 Oct 1951. NOTE: no periods or commas are used. Months may be written in all capital letters or upper and lower case, and should be reduced to three letters except for June, since

# PEDIGREE CHART #_____

Chart no. _____

Person #1 is same person as #_____ on chart #_____

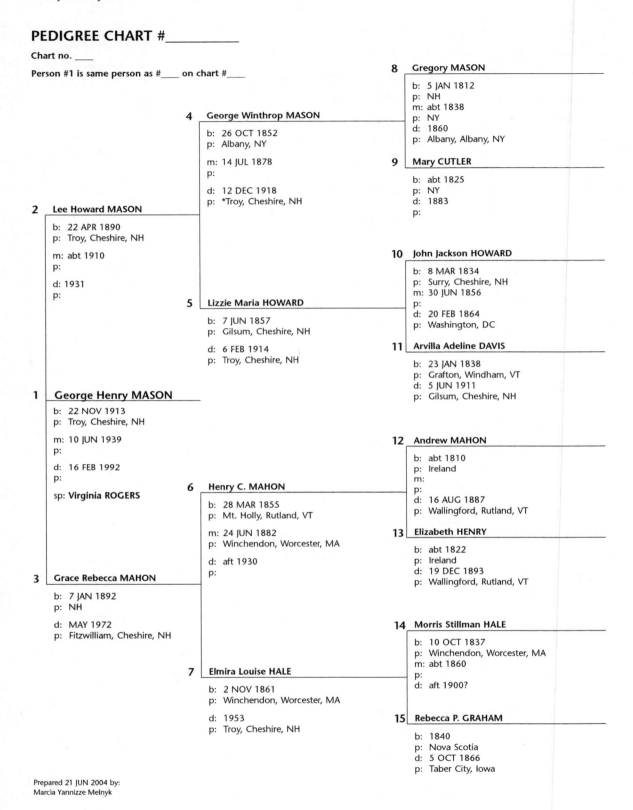

**8 Gregory MASON**

b: 5 JAN 1812
p: NH
m: abt 1838
p: NY
d: 1860
p: Albany, Albany, NY

**4 George Winthrop MASON**

b: 26 OCT 1852
p: Albany, NY

m: 14 JUL 1878
p:

d: 12 DEC 1918
p: *Troy, Cheshire, NH

**9 Mary CUTLER**

b: abt 1825
p: NY
d: 1883
p:

**2 Lee Howard MASON**

b: 22 APR 1890
p: Troy, Cheshire, NH

m: abt 1910
p:

d: 1931
p:

**10 John Jackson HOWARD**

b: 8 MAR 1834
p: Surry, Cheshire, NH
m: 30 JUN 1856
p:
d: 20 FEB 1864
p: Washington, DC

**5 Lizzie Maria HOWARD**

b: 7 JUN 1857
p: Gilsum, Cheshire, NH

d: 6 FEB 1914
p: Troy, Cheshire, NH

**11 Arvilla Adeline DAVIS**

b: 23 JAN 1838
p: Grafton, Windham, VT
d: 5 JUN 1911
p: Gilsum, Cheshire, NH

**1   George Henry MASON**

b: 22 NOV 1913
p: Troy, Cheshire, NH

m: 10 JUN 1939
p:

d: 16 FEB 1992
p:

sp: **Virginia ROGERS**

**12 Andrew MAHON**

b: abt 1810
p: Ireland
m:
p:
d: 16 AUG 1887
p: Wallingford, Rutland, VT

**6 Henry C. MAHON**

b: 28 MAR 1855
p: Mt. Holly, Rutland, VT

m: 24 JUN 1882
p: Winchendon, Worcester, MA

d: aft 1930
p:

**13 Elizabeth HENRY**

b: abt 1822
p: Ireland
d: 19 DEC 1893
p: Wallingford, Rutland, VT

**3 Grace Rebecca MAHON**

b: 7 JAN 1892
p: NH

d: MAY 1972
p: Fitzwilliam, Cheshire, NH

**14 Morris Stillman HALE**

b: 10 OCT 1837
p: Winchendon, Worcester, MA
m: abt 1860
p:
d: aft 1900?

**7 Elmira Louise HALE**

b: 2 NOV 1861
p: Winchendon, Worcester, MA

d: 1953
p: Troy, Cheshire, NH

**15 Rebecca P. GRAHAM**

b: 1840
p: Nova Scotia
d: 5 OCT 1866
p: Taber City, Iowa

Prepared 21 JUN 2004 by:
Marcia Yannizze Melnyk

**Figure 3-1**
Pedigree chart for George Henry Mason.

# FAMILY GROUP SHEET

| HUSBAND | | *Lee Howard* MASON | |
|---|---|---|---|
| | **Birth** | 22 APR 1890 | Troy, Cheshire, NH |
| | **Census** | 1930 | Lebanon, Grafton, NH [1] |
| | **Death** | 1931 | |
| | **Census (fam)** | 1910 | Troy. Cheshire. NH [2] |
| | **Marriage** | abt 1910 | |
| | **Census (fam)** | 1920 | Troy. Cheshire. NH [3] |
| | **Father** | George Winthrop MASON (1852–1918) | |
| | **Mother** | Lizzie Maria HOWARD (1857–1914) | |

| Wife | | *Grace Rebecca* MAHON | |
|---|---|---|---|
| | **Birth** | 7 JAN 1892 | NH |
| | **Death** | MAY 1972 | Fitzwilliam. Cheshire. NH |
| | **Father** | Henry C. MAHON (1855–1930) | |
| | **Mother** | Elmira Louise HALE (1861–1953) | |
| | **Other spouse** | BICKFORD ( – ) | |
| | **Marriage** | aft 1931 | |

### Children

| 1 F | Geraldine MASON | |
|---|---|---|
| | **Birth** | abt 1912 | Troy. Cheshire. NH |

| 2 M | George Henry MASON | |
|---|---|---|
| | **Birth** | 22 NOV 1913 | Troy. Cheshire. NH |
| | **Death** | 16 FEB 1992 | |
| | **Spouse** | Virginia ROGERS (1916– ) | |
| | **Marriage** | 10 JUN 1939 | |

| Prepared 21 JUN 2004 by: Marcia Yannizze Melnyk | Comments |
|---|---|

### FAMILY NOTES

**Census (fam): 1910 US Census; NH, Cheshire Col, Troy; ED#47; sheet 1A; family #2/2**
MASON, George W.; head; male; white; 57y; m/1 for 31y; b NY; father b NH; mother b NY; salesman/grocery store
MASON, Lizzie M.; wife; female; white; 52y; m/1 for 31y; b NH; father b NH; mother b NH; mother of 4 children/2 living
ROCKWOOD, Ina M.; daughter; female; white; 27y; m/1 for 7 months; born NH; father b NH; mother b NH
ROCKWOOD, Claude E.; son-in-law; male; white; 33y; m/1 for 7 months; b NH; father b NH; mother b VT; cord weaver/blanket mill
MASON, Lee H.; son; male; white; 19y; single; b NH; father b NY; mother b NH
**Census (fam): 1920; NH, Cheshire Co., Troy; S. Main St.; ED#22; pg 12A**
MASON, Lee H.; head; male; white; 29y; married; b NH; father b NY; mother b NY: laborer in blanket mill
MASON, Grace R.; wife; female; white; 28y; married; b NH; father b NH; mother b Nova Scotia
MASON, Geraldine; daughter; female; white; 8y; single; b NH; father b NH; mother b NH
MASON, George; son; male; white; 6y; single; b NH; father b NH; mother b NH

### HUSBAND NOTES: LEE HOWARD MASON

**Census: 1930 US Census: Lebanon, Grafton Co., NH; ED#5-25; pg 14A**
MASON, Lee; 38y; boarder; male; white; m/20 yrs; b NH; father b NY; mother b NH; painter/self-employed

### SOURCES

1. NARA, T626; roll 1300; ED#5-25; pg 14A.
2. Ibid, T624; roll 861; ED#47; pg 1A.
3. Ibid, T625; roll 1006; ED#22; pg 12A.

**Figure 3-2**
Family Group Sheet for the Lee Howard Mason family.

**Notes**

**COMMON ABBREVIATIONS**

b = born

bpt = baptised

bur = buried

d = died

dod = date of death

m = married

pob = place of birth

pod = place of death

pom = place of marriage

Jan and Jun can be misread when handwritten (unless capital letters are used).

- *Observe standard abbreviations used in recording genealogical data.*
- *Place names should always be listed from the smallest geographic location to the largest: Town, County, State, Country.* Most other countries have similar breakdowns in their locations. For example, in Italy they are called comune (town), provincia (county), and regione (state), and would be recorded in that order.

> EXAMPLE: Concord, Middlesex, MA. In recording place names, always spell out the town or city names. You can reduce the county to five or six letters by omitting the vowels. Use postal abbreviations for states, and place commas between each location.

It is important to look up and always list the county at the time of an event, as well as any geographic divisions that may have occurred over time. You may find records at any of the governmental levels, and knowing the names of the counties, as well as how that county's boundaries may have changed through time—perhaps placing the records somewhere unexpected—is crucial.

## ADDITIONAL FORMS

*Research logs* are vital to your family history search. **A research log keeps track of all the sources you have used in your research for a given subject or family.** If you keep one for each surname, you can prevent duplication of your research time as well as retrace your steps if needed. List the books, vital records, etc. that you've searched, their location, and the results of that search. Log the source even if you found nothing—it will prevent you from revisiting a dead end! (See Figure 3-3 on page 31.)

I list the books I want to look at in a library directly from the card catalog onto my research log. This saves me the step of recording it later. It also prevents me from forgetting to list unsuccessful research. By listing the book (including the call number, author, title, publication date, edition, and publisher) before I look at it, I can then record "nothing found" or "incorrect family" to prevent me from looking at that book again and again. Knowing the publication date can alert you to second or third editions that may contain new, different, or corrected information.

You can keep your research logs by family, surname, location, reposi-

\di'fin\ *vb*

Definitions

## RESEARCH CALENDAR
*Note the records you've checked for ancestral clues*

RESEARCHER _____ ANCESTOR _____

LOCALITY _____ TIME PERIOD _____

BRIEF PROBLEM STATEMENT _____

| Search Date | Where Available | Call# | Title/Author/Publisher/Year or Record Identification Info | Notes | Page #s |
|---|---|---|---|---|---|
| | | | | | |
| | | | | | |
| | | | | | |
| | | | | | |
| | | | | | |
| | | | | | |
| | | | | | |
| | | | | | |
| | | | | | |
| | | | | | |
| | | | | | |
| | | | | | |
| | | | | | |
| | | | | | |
| | | | | | |
| | | | | | |
| | | | | | |
| | | | | | |
| | | | | | |

**Figure 3-3**
Research Calendar.

tory, or whatever works for you. Just be consistent and record everything you look at regardless of the results!

There are *customized forms* of different styles to use to record data as you find it. You can purchase these or make them yourself. They include forms to record land, probate, census, obituary, cemetery, and other records. Many genealogical supply companies produce them. I've also made many forms on my computer. Having a standard form helps prevent missed information and can save you money when certified copies aren't needed.

Many times when you purchase a certified copy of a record from a town, county, or state office, the clerk will fill the information in on their standard form. The problem with this is there is sometimes more information on the original record than you will get transcribed to their form. If there is no space on the form they're using for all the information, they do not fill it in. Think about filling in a form. Do you provide answers to questions that are not asked? Many times an "official" death certificate eliminates the informant's name or relationship to the deceased, for example. This is important information to the genealogical researcher, whereas sometimes it is irrelevant when the document is needed for other purposes. You want all the information, not selected bits. Always be careful of records marked "selected records." This indicates that there is more information but someone has "selected" what he or she thinks is important. Once you have used a particular type of record that you will be using again and again, you can create a form specific to the record. In this way you're less likely to miss information, and it makes transcribing or abstracting the record more efficient.

Some of the many forms I have created over the years were customized to the records I was using. Whenever you encounter an index for a record you'll be using, create a form using the exact layout of the index. This makes using the records more efficient. You can easily extract information from the index onto your form. Then, when you go to view the actual records, you can check them off as you look at them.

An example of this is the Massachusetts vital records indexes. The indexes are set up in five-year categories as follows:

| Surname | Given Name | Town Reporting | Year | Volume | Page # |
|---------|------------|----------------|------|--------|--------|
| BRUNO | John | Saugus | 1923 | 215 | 325 |

As you can see below, to create the form that included all of the information I wanted, I also added the necessary column for the event, since the indexes for birth, marriages, and deaths are all in separate volumes. By setting up a form with these six columns and adding an additional column for notations, you can quickly record the information you'll need later. The form might look like this:

| Surname | Given Name | Town | Year | Event | Vol. & pg. | Results |
|---------|-----------|------|------|-------|-----------|---------|
| BRUNO | John | Saugus | 1923 | death | 215:325 | checked |
| BRUNO | Bridget | Saugus | 1921 | death | 175:410 | got copy |

Tip

**You can also create a form that matches the actual document to make copying the information easier.** Since paying for certified copies can get expensive, I prefer to hand-copy the information unless I am required to purchase a certificate. You can also arrange your form in a different format than the actual record, including all of the information that might appear on the record, in an arrangement that suits you better. This is handy when the record forms change over a period of time and you don't want to create a lot of different forms.

Another form I use quite frequently is a city directory log sheet. I find a form makes the transcription of data easier, which is very convenient since I do a lot of research in cities and towns during the period when directories were in use. By using one form for each individual over a number of years, I can see the information as an overview of multiple years rather than just a single year. The form might look like this:

| Year | City | Name | Spouse | Employed @ | Residence @ | Misc. info |
|------|------|------|--------|-----------|-------------|-----------|
| 1920 | Saugus | BRUNO, John | Bridgida | carpenter | h@33 Bristow | |
| 1920 | Saugus | BRUNO, John | ------ | laborer | b@33 Bristow | *Gennaro Jr.* |

While forms for extracting information will help you focus all of the information on one piece of paper, there are some records it's better to have a copy of than a form with extracted information. Census records are one such item. While you can get forms for extracting the information in any given census year, making a copy of the actual census page is more efficient. Why? Because of all of the columns, information, and the possibility of missing some of the clues that appear in neighboring families. If the family you're researching appears at the top or the bottom of the page, I recommend copying the previous/next page as well. I've found many relatives I was not looking for by employing this method.

Once you've made copies of the actual census image, you can use a form to extract the data you want to compare to another census year, then compile the results onto another form. You now have an overview of the family over several decades, but still have the actual census records to look back to (see Figure 3-4 on page 35).

I also created a form for copying down information contained on the index cards for census and naturalization records. Again, I made a copy of the actual index cards and then made a form following the format to make extracting easier. This way, I can do all of my extracting at once and then go to the census or naturalization records. When I find the record that matches the card, I can either make a copy and staple the form to it or write my notes right on the form, indicating why I didn't make a copy (e.g. wrong family or individual, etc.). By doing this, I not only have a record of every document I looked at, but I have a complete citation for the ones I copied.

Forms can be made using Microsoft Excel, by inserting a table into a Microsoft Word document, or by using a special program to create them. You can even create them with just a ruler! I have used all these ways to create custom forms but prefer a form-creating program. I use Cosmi Forms Maker & Filler (sometimes marketed under the Swift name). It costs under $30 and you should be able to get it at software stores or online at <www.cosmi.com>.

## Utilizing Existing Forms

Once you begin thinking about forms you'll be amazed at all the types that are available in office supply stores, books, online, etc. There is a wonderful book by Emily Anne Croom called *The Unpuzzling Your Past Workbook* that provides you with more than forty forms to photocopy and use, as well as many ideas and suggestions of creative ways to use them. Find out what works for you and what doesn't, and then customize a form that suits your needs.

**Reminder**

**Many "how-to" books have some forms included in them.** This is especially true of the genealogical books published by Family Tree Books, formerly Betterway Books. *A Genealogist's Guide to Discovering Your Italian Ancestors* by Lynn Nelson, for example, contains wonderful extraction forms for recording what you find on the microfilmed Italian records.

Keep an eye out for other types of forms, and be creative in making

## CENSUS OVERVIEW FORM

Name: b place m place d place s/o

Name: b place m place d place d/o

| YEAR/ROLL # | INFORMATION FOUND | SEARCHED | FOUND IN |
|---|---|---|---|
| | | | |
| | | | |
| | | | |
| | | | |
| | | | |

**Figure 3-4**
Census overview form.

your own. Try to purchase archival paper or forms whenever possible. Many of the genealogical suppliers sell acid-free forms. Since you want your research to last, be sure to record your permanent data on acid-free forms designed specifically for longevity. Trial and error will show you what you need and what you will use.

## ORGANIZING YOUR RESEARCH

As you acquire documents, notes, records, forms, and correspondence, you need to keep it accessible for quick reference. Creating a system that works for you will make the records retrievable when you need them and easily filed when you are finished. Making your research efficient by staying organized will make you a better and more thorough researcher.

The system I use consists of the following:

1. **Binders that are color-coded on the spines with dots.** Surnames within the binder are alphabetical and contain all generations of that family name. Tabbed dividers separate each surname. Each divider tab is also coded with the same color dot as the binder, to indicate where it belongs. Along with the family group sheets, I also put abstracts of deeds, notes, etc. that may be used for reference while researching. This sometimes includes notes on the collateral lines of that family that may help identify other relatives.

2. **An alphabetical card index of all surnames that appear on my pedigree charts.** Each card contains the surname, lineage, and pertinent information—

---

### SUPPLY LIST

Supply list for organizing your files and research—most are available at office supply stores:

- index cards (3″ × 5″ or 4″ × 6″)

- 3-hole punch (best to get one that converts to 2-hole)

- three-ring binders

- dividers for three-ring binders (one divider for each surname)

- colored dots (large and small sizes)

- hanging file folders with labels

- maps of research states (see *Ancestry's Red Book* for great maps)

- blank forms (pedigree, family group, census overview, etc.)

such as dates and locations. The card contains the color coding dot and the pedigree chart numbers that the surname appears on. (See Figure 3-1 for a sample card on page 28.)

3. **Binders (or files) that hold backup documents.** These binders or files contain all the copies of certificates, documents, and papers pertaining to a specific person or family. They can be divided by family name, by specific couples, generations, or whatever works for you. When I get a land, probate, or other lengthy handwritten document, I actually do a complete transcription onto the computer. I print it out and staple the typed copy to the handwritten document and file it. I can then add an abstract to the family group sheets in the correct binder. **This makes reviewing the documents later more efficient as you don't have to reacquaint yourself with the handwriting or decipher it again.** When you are transcribing several records from the same location, they're easier to read because you become accustomed to the format, handwriting, and terminology used. The typed document is also much easier to reference later, after you're away from the idiosyncrasies of the original documents for awhile.

Tip

I created my hanging files by dividing them by the couples as they appear on my pedigree charts (remember the lineal ancestors?). I label one file for each generation (husband and wife's names) and keep all records pertaining to that family (including all their children) in the parents' folder. The one child of this couple that I descend from then has his or her own folder. I leave all records for that child before his or her marriage in the parent's folder. Once an ancestor marries, their records go into their own file and no longer into the parent's. This means that I would have as many ROGERS folders as I have generations listed on the pedigree chart. They would be labeled as follows:

ROGERS, Seneca and Diana ROUNDS (my grandparents)

ROGERS, Hoxey and Teresa EMERY (my great-grandparents)

ROGERS, Joseph and Anna BARBER (my great-great-grandparents)

ROGERS, Constant and Love CUMMINGS (my great-great-great-grandparents)

ROGERS, Samuel and Mehitable HUBBARD (my great-great-great-great-grandparents)

This way, all of the ROGERS generations are grouped together in the file drawer in order of generation. Seneca is the last male in the ROGERS line, being my maternal grandfather. The only record that is duplicated in this system is the marriage record for Seneca ROGERS and Diana ROUNDS, which would be filed in the following three places:

1. the "ROGERS, Seneca and Diana ROUNDS" file
2. the "ROGERS, Hoxey and Teresa EMERY" (Seneca's parents)
3. the "ROUNDS, Orville and Ella Mae BISSONETTE" (Diana's parents)

By using this method, I always have a cross reference to the bride's parents and always know where to find any given record. You'll want to design your files to suit your personal style. There is no right or wrong method as long as it has a logical format that you will be able to use and keep up with.

4. **Travel binders for research trips to specific locations.** These binders hold information regarding the research facilities or geographic area that I may need on a research trip. This binder should be the loudest, most obnoxious color you can find. I once lost a black binder in a library—I think someone else picked it up thinking it was theirs. Even though my name was inside the cover and on every divider inside, it was never returned to me. Since that day I always use a florescent orange or green binder for research trips. I then insert the families I will be researching by removing them from the appropriate binder (along with the color-coded divider). I also include a research checklist or list of objectives for those families to help me focus my research. I always review what I have when deciding which objectives to set, and this helps familiarize me with the previous research that I've done. I always carry blank copies of frequently used forms (like pedigree, family group, vital records extraction, and research log forms) in these binders. Since almost all facilities have photocopiers, you can carry just a couple of each form and make copies as you need them. Upon returning home I can easily transfer the new information to my computer database and to the family group sheets, and refile the family I was working on in their specific binder by using the color coded dots.

5. **Copies for backup or travel.** I keep copies (two paper copies or disk backups kept at different locations) of all of my pedigree charts and computer databases. I keep a travel copy of my pedigrees that I can mark up when I am researching and then transfer the data to the computer database when I get home. **If you travel with a laptop computer, make sure your database is copied and left at home or with a friend.** Don't ever take your only copy or originals of anything with you. Carry as little paper with you as

**Important**

possible. By planning ahead and carrying only what you need, you'll spend less time leafing through your binders looking for information.

## Research Tips to Keep You Organized

1. Whenever you make photocopies from a book, always remember to copy the title and publication pages first (the ones containing the date of publication, publisher's name, and copyright information), then the pages that pertain to your research. I list the pages I need to copy on an index card. Don't use little slips of paper to mark the pages you want to copy. They can fall out of the book and you'll miss those pages when making the copies. After copying all the pages listed on my index card I write the call number and library (or facility location) on the title page if it is not already there. I then highlight the information that I need on each page. This way you'll catch mistakes (like copying the wrong page in the book) immediately and not when you get home. I have, at times, forgotten why I copied a certain page upon returning home. Photocopies are cheap insurance when you are researching far from home. Staple all copies together and move on to the next book. Don't spend time transcribing the data on location. If you use a laptop computer don't type in the information rather than make copies. When you get home and find that you missed a piece of information or dates don't look correct, you won't know if the original was incorrect or if you transcribed or typed it incorrectly. With photocopies there is no doubt and you can always reference them later. You're also spending valuable time transcribing when you could be researching.

2. Use your research logs faithfully. I use mine to record the call numbers, title, etc. of every book I look at (not only the ones I find something in). Negative results must still be documented so you will not repeat the research.

3. Use spiral bound notebooks, not loose paper, when taking notes. I use specific notebooks for specific family groups. When I enter a facility the first thing I do is turn to the first empty page, date it, and note what facility I'm at. That way, all of my notes will pertain to that facility until I encounter another dated page. Make sure that all notebooks are labeled with your name and address. Self-stick address labels are great for this. Sticky notes and blank index cards can be used to make notes of things you want to look up later. Keep them all together and refer to them as needed.

4. Make sure that you know the rules of the research facility. Some don't allow you to take in notebooks, briefcases, etc. If you know this ahead of time, you can put your research objectives on index cards that will fit in

your pocket. Some will let you take in note pads and small notebooks. Plan ahead! Knowing how much copies cost, available lunch facilities, research restrictions, etc. can make for a more efficient trip.

5. If possible, do all of your indexing ahead of time (from microfilm or books available locally). You can then devote more time to the actual records at the facility. Many have short hours, uncomfortable accommodations, and busy clerks. If you cannot index prior to going, do the indexing first. Check the index for all names while you have it. This is where an alphabetical list comes in handy. You can just run down the list of names. I have found ancestors in places I never expected to find them by doing this.

6. **Keep maps of the states your ancestors lived in with your research binders.** Add them to your traveling binder after deciding your research strategies. I often use the ones in *Ancestry's Red Book* (at the end of each chapter) because they also show the counties and towns bordering the specific state. Geographic proximity can be an important piece of information. Unless you're familiar with the area, you might not know which towns or counties abut your ancestor's locale. It is important to know the nearby town or county names when using indexes to determine which records are more likely to pertain to your research. I use simple outline maps with the towns and counties labeled. I highlight the towns where my ancestors were known to have resided or done business. A quick look at the map tells me that the John Rogers who left a record in Columbia, Tolland County, Connecticut, might be the same John Rogers who lived in Lebanon, New London County, Connecticut, since the towns are next to each other. The same applies to towns located on state lines. You may have to look in another state's records as well. Always keep the geographic location in mind.

**Tip**

You can find state maps with county designations in *Map Guide to the U.S. Federal Censuses, 1790–1920*, by William Dollarhide and William Thorndale (Baltimore: Genealogical Publishing Company, 2000), *The Family Tree Resource Book for Genealogists*, edited by Sharon DeBartolo Carmack and Erin Nevius (Cincinnati: Family Tree Books, 2004), and *The Handybook for Genealogists: United States of America, 10th Edition* (Logan, Utah: Everton Publishers, 2002).

## ALPHABETICAL SURNAME FILE

My alphabetical surname file is on index cards that are set up like a Rolodex. The cards are punched at the bottom (two holes) and connected with book rings available at office supply stores. This keeps them together even if you drop them. Each card contains the pedigree or lineage of one surname only (see Figure 3-5 on page 41). The card duplicates the labels of the hanging files previously mentioned. Think of the card as a stairway to the past. The generation closest to you should be at the bottom of the stairway (usually a female, as the surname ends there). When you discover the parents of that person, add them on the next line up. The further up the "stairway" you go, the further back in time you are. Eight or nine generations can fit on one card. I always take these cards with me wherever I go. Even if you don't plan to research all lines, you never know when those names will pop up in a book or record. The information contained on the card should refer only to the person with that surname. The wife of the person (e.g. Malona Carpenter, wife of Spencer Rounds) will appear on the "Carpenter" card with all her information. This way you always have a cross-reference to the married name of any female.

| **Rounds** | | | **R532 (Soundex Code)** |
|---|---|---|---|
| George | (c1686-c1765) | m Susanna COLE | c 1713 MA |
| James | (1722-1787) | m Susanna SEAMANS | 1741 MA |
| Joseph | (1775-1831) | m Phebe RENSLOW | c 1795 VT/NY |
| | | or MILLINGTON | |
| Linus | (c1798-1875) | m Hannah WESCOTT | c 1820 VT? |
| Spencer | (1833-1906) | m Malona CARPENTER | c 1860 VT |
| Orville | (1871-1948) | m Ella Mae BISSONETTE | 1890 VT |
| Diana Belle | (1892-1941) | m Seneca Baker ROGERS | 1913 NH |

○ = colored dot indicating "home spot binder"          pedigree chart #'s 1, 6, 42

**Figure 3-5**
Sample of a completed surname index card.

## THE RESEARCH PLAN

One last form or list you should use is a research plan form. Review your previous research before you leave home and list the items you need to get or verify. This will help you stay focused on your goals while researching. It's so easy to get sidetracked when you come across unexpected information. Review your list of goals several times during any research trip to remind yourself what you planned to do. This doesn't mean that you can't change your direction should you find an unexpected source, but you *can* weigh the importance of one goal over the other.

I sometimes write my research goals on index cards. This works well when you are working with census records. If possible, I look at the census records online at one of the sites that have indexes and/or images. Since I always get a copy of every census record for my family, I use the online image to determine if it is the correct family. I then list the head of household, state, county, ED# (enumeration district) if applicable, page number, and line number on the index card, along with the film series number and the microfilm roll number.

When I get to the National Archives facility to get copies of the census images, I take the card, pull the roll of film, go directly to the actual page, and print it. I then staple the index card to the photocopies. This provides me with my complete citation for entering the data later onto my forms or into my database (see Figure 3-6 below). Because the head of household's name is at the top of the card, I can also place the copy easily into the proper file.

**Figure 3-6**
Sample of a citation index card.

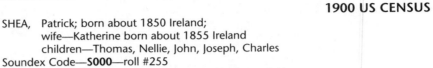

**1900 US CENSUS**

SHEA,   Patrick; born about 1850 Ireland;
           wife—Katherine born about 1855 Ireland
           children—Thomas, Nellie, John, Joseph, Charles
Soundex Code—**S000**—roll #255
MA, Suffolk Co., Boston, Precinct #4; ED# 1281; page 6A
Census—Series T623—Roll #679

Now that you are acquainted with some of the many forms available to researchers and have a filing system laid out, you can begin to prove or disprove the facts. Some people are surprised at how much they've accumulated at this stage in their research. This is especially true if other family members have given you Great Aunt Edith's genealogical research. They're probably glad to have found an interested party to give it to.

Warning

**The information from anyone else's research should not be incorporated into your records until the data has been proven.** Unfortunately, most of the research done in the early 1900s bears few sources or verification of facts. But look at the bright side. At least you have names to work from and perhaps the maiden names of some of your great-grandmothers—it's a start!

# FOUR

# Surfing the Web

The Internet, e-mail, computerized databases, and CD-ROMs have drastically changed genealogical research over the last twenty or so years—not always for the better. Use of these electronic tools can make locating "relatives" (both living and dead) as easy as a click of the mouse. Web sites abound with family trees, pedigrees, stories, photos, etc. While there are still some people who believe that all the answers they need are on the Internet, the seasoned researcher knows better. The immense body of records created by our ancestors includes millions of pages of paper records, thousands of rolls of microfilm, books and manuscripts, etc. To digitize (put into electronic format) this body of records would be an almost impossible task. Records are being indexed, scanned, or microfilmed every day, but I don't think we'll live long enough to see the day when all records are available online.

**You need to be cautious—just because the information comes off a computer does not make it true.** Just as in printed genealogies and other books, there are many unproven facts and assumptions flying around in cyberspace. When poor research is posted on the Internet, it is likely to be duplicated, reposted, and otherwise taken as fact. This poses a unique problem if you are new to research. We're all happy to find that someone else has done some research on our family line. We get excited when we find multiple generations posted on a Web site. The temptation is to take it and run with it. But before we incorporate it into our family tree, we must dissect the information just as ruthlessly as we do any other source. Do the facts fit the individuals involved? Does the Web site present any source material? Where did the information come from? If there are no sources listed, use

Warning

the information gleaned from the family pedigrees, record extractions, and indexes posted on the site for what it is—secondhand or secondary information, which may or may not be correct.

---

### QUESTIONS TO ASK OF EVERY DATABASE

- How was it created—was the data transcribed or was the actual record scanned?

- Are the sources used to compile the database listed?

- Were those sources primary or secondary ones?

- Are sources cited for each fact?

- Does the database or CD offer tips for effective searching?

---

Now that you've been warned, let's move on to the different types of computerized records available and how you can best utilize them.

## THE GOOD

The Internet has made many good and reliable sources of information easily available. Web sites such as the following are well worth a visit.

### Free Web Sites

There are several important free sites that will provide you with more links to other sites than you will know what to do with at first. By approaching your computer research in the same manner as library or archive research, you'll have better control and not become so overwhelmed. Allow yourself time to play with a few important genealogical sites and get to know how

---

### TERMS AND ABBREVIATIONS

CD-ROM—Compact Disk Read-Only Memory

Database—compiled collection of records in an electronic format

IGI—International Genealogical Index

ISP—Internet Service Provider

URL—Uniform Resource Locator (address)

---

they work, what they offer, and how to best navigate them. As with any type of research, remember to keep a research log!

**Some of the free Web sites that every family historian needs to know about are:**

Internet Source

### Cyndi's List

<www.cyndislist.com>

This Web site is subject-based, meaning that you can search for information by locality, subject matter, era, etc. While this site has no records posted, it has over two hundred thousand links to other sites of genealogical and historical interest. I use Cyndi's List whenever I approach a new type of record or a new locality in my research. By typing either a locality or subject into the search box, you'll get a list of sites that have information specific to that search.

The list that will come up (after your search) will contain many sites, but you're interested in the one labeled "Cyndi's List." Click on that title and you'll be taken to another page that lists subcategories within the context of your subject matter. You can find libraries, societies, history, culture, and much more.

Even the home page for Cyndi's List offers many opportunities to learn. Take the time to read the information in "What is Cyndi's List?," "Are You New to Genealogy?," "Frequently Asked Questions," and "Internet Stuff You Need to Know" before you venture any further.

Once you feel comfortable with using Cyndi's List and the links, you'll be able to come up with dozens of categories that you can use for your research.

### USGenWeb

<www.usgenweb.org>

This site is based mostly on locality. You can find links to state, county, and sometimes local sites. The USGenWeb has one volunteer-staffed site for each county within the United States. These sites may vary greatly as to their content, look, and the number of records available to search, but do offer some unique information that many researchers tend to overlook.

Once you click on the state link you will find information relative to state records, vital records, state libraries, and other state resources. Many of the state pages offer an overview of the history of the state and counties, information about the availability of certain types of records, and will provide links to the county sites within the given state. Many of these sites also offer articles about researching in that state, with some providing printable research guides that will assist you.

After you have reviewed the state page, click on the county you're interested in. You will then find a myriad of information links. Some of the county or town sites actually have a list of volunteers who will do lookups for you. **The lookup volunteers will often list the books or records that they are willing to look at—perhaps books that they own or have easy access to.** This information is valuable if you are unfamiliar with the local resources available. If there is a book listed on the site, you can then look for it in a library close to you, or perhaps borrow it by interlibrary loan. Interlibrary loan is an extremely helpful service offered by many libraries in which a library requests material from, or supplies material to, another library. Check with your local library to find out if it's available.

Knowing the titles of locally published books, manuscripts, and histories makes it easier to locate them outside of the area they cover. Many of the local historical or genealogical societies publish books or lists of records, cemetery inscriptions, etc. that can be valuable to any researcher. The sites also offer places to post online queries regarding research or specific individuals for whom you are searching. I've made contact with many other researchers who have information on my lines by posting a question or query on such sites.

Another link from the county sites will guide you to local historical and genealogical societies. I've always found it useful to join these local societies when I am researching in an unfamiliar state or county. Doing so will put you in touch with the people who know the area, the history, and the unique records that might be available. Most societies offer services to members that may include free look-ups, free queries posted in their newsletters, discounts on published materials, etc. It never hurts to check out these offerings.

### Rootsweb

<www.rootsweb.com>

This site is mostly surname-based, but does include some locality-based links. RootsWeb.com also offers a weekly newsletter containing information, instruction, and links to other sites that will be useful to you. There are many opportunities to learn from any site you visit, and you never know what you'll find. I found a photograph of a gravesite on the Roots-

**Money Saver**

Web.com cemetery project pages that provided previously unknown birth and death dates.

New material is added all the time, so you must recheck this network of sites often to see what other resources might be available. Networking is probably the most amazing thing about the Internet. Posting questions on any of the free Web sites can bring researchers with similar interests or valuable knowledge to you. I've even made contact with relatives via one of the message boards. The idea is to get your name and research interests out there so that others may find you.

### FamilySearch
### <www.familysearch.org>

This Web site has just about everything a researcher could hope for. It was created and is maintained by the Church of Jesus Christ of Latter-day Saints (also called Mormons). The site has many useful databases, some more questionable than others. Some of the offerings include the IGI (International Genealogical Index), Ancestral File (linked pedigrees), Census (1880 U.S.; 1881 Great Britain, and 1881 Canada), and Social Security Death Index, to name a few.

The home page has three categories from which to choose. These are *Search for Ancestors, Share Information*, and *Family History Library System*. Under the *Search for Ancestors* heading, you'll find articles about doing research, research guides, maps, forms, and databases that you can search. I always go here when I begin a new research subject. Look for a guide specific to the subject matter or geographical place you'll be researching. The guides will give you a good overview of what is available, both through the Family History Library System and in the native country (if overseas) or state of interest. Again, knowing what to expect will go a long way in your search.

**Many of the foreign country resource guides include exceptional word lists.** After I used an Italian-English dictionary, not always successfully, I found the FamilySearch online word list and I'm still using it to this day, along with a much better Italian-English dictionary. The important thing about the word lists offered at FamilySearch is that they contain words you'll encounter in records. So many words are no longer used or have a specific meaning when used in the context of birth, marriage, death, or other records.

Under *Family History Library System* (we will cover the *Share Information* heading in chapter ten), you can learn about the library system or find a Family History Center (regional branches of the Salt Lake City Family

Sources

History Library) near you. With thousands of these Family History Centers (FHC) around the world, you should be able to find one in your area.

You can also search online for microfilmed records from every corner of the globe. In the Family History Library Catalog you can search by place, surname, key word, title, author, subject, etc. While the books do not circulate out of the main library in Salt Lake City, many have been microfilmed and are available through the FHC in your area. If the book hasn't been filmed you can try to find it in your local library or through interlibrary loan. Again, knowing that a book exists is half the battle. Once you've found a microfilm, you can order it for a nominal fee for use at one of the FHCs. The film is rented for a specific time period but you can renew it (for an additional fee) until you've completed your research. I find this to be valuable when dealing with foreign records. They are time-consuming to go through since you will not only have bad handwriting and faded ink to deal with, but a foreign language as well!

## Subscription Web Sites

Now that we've covered the free sites, let's look at the sites that charge for access to their large databases of records.

### Ancestry, Inc.
<www.ancestry.com>

This site contains over seven hundred databases to search; a daily newsletter listing new databases, articles, and news of importance to researchers; instructional articles; information about other sites; and more.

The databases include such helpful research aids as indexes and images of census records (United States, Great Britain, Canada, Wales, Isle of Man, etc.), newspapers, vital and land records, directories, military pensions, burials, draft registrations, the Social Security Death Index, and more.

Ancestry offers many different subscription options, so you'll need to determine which will be the most useful for you. Go to the site, search on a name, and see what comes up. A list will appear that tells you in which databases the name was found. Look over the list and take note of the databases—these may be the most beneficial to subscribe to. If you get only a few hits, perhaps this database site is not the best for your research. I've found little other than the Social Security Death Index that helped with my recent immigrant ancestors, but it is a wonderful resource for my mother's English and colonial ancestors.

**Check your local or genealogical society library, as well as the National Archives facilities, to see if they have subscriptions to any of Ancestry's databases.** Many have access to the Internet and subscriptions that you can use for free at the facility.

### Genealogy.com and Family Tree Maker
<www.familytreemaker.com> or <www.genealogy.com>

These sites have been combined and either address (at this time) will take you to the same databases. They contain researcher-submitted pedigrees, instructional articles, census records, family and local histories, international and passenger records, data on the Family Tree Maker CD-ROM collections. Like the Ancestry.com Web site, you should determine if the selection of databases is useful to your research before subscribing. If a genealogical library owns copies of the World Family Tree CD-ROM series, you can use the Web site to determine which disks you need to look at before you go to the library. Use the search features on the site to determine which databases your ancestor appears in, and then decide if buying a subscription is worthwhile.

This site, as mentioned before, has wonderful how-to articles that are of great assistance to any researcher. The Learning Center is free and the databases may be accessed through several different database subscriptions.

## Search Engines

When using search engines, keep in mind that new ones are always popping up and they will all produce different results. Use different ones to see what discrepancies and additional information you can find. There are many search engines, including <www.google.com>, <www.dogpile.com>, <www.lycos.com>, <www.altavista.com>, and <www.yahoo.com>. Some of these access other search engines in their searches, saving you time and effort by combining the results of multiple search engines for you. Many search engines offer tips on how to do simple and advanced searches. It's well worth the time to read these help pages to get the most out of that search engine.

Search engines can be compared to the online card catalogs at many libraries. Rather than indexing books specifically, they index the millions of Web sites out there in cyberspace. Trial and error will tell you which ones work best for you, but it's always a good idea to do the same searches on several different engines just to compare the results.

There are a few different tricks and techniques to try in order to get the most specific, valuable results. If your search includes a common name or word, you may get too many hits to sort through. Try putting the name or phrase in quotation marks (e.g. "Shirley Lampere"). This tells the search engine that you want the two words to appear in that specific order and will eliminate all of the hits that just contain one of the two words. You can also try adding a modifier to the search. This means that you could type in: "Shirley Lampere" + Vermont. This will present options referring to Shirley Lampere in the state of Vermont. Play around with different combinations and see what results. Remember that this is a learning process.

Whenever you encounter a URL, look at the extension at the end of the address. United States-based Web sites will have different extensions at the end of the address. A .com is a commercial site, .org is a nonprofit organization, .net is a network, .edu is an educational facility, and .gov is a government Web site. Foreign Web sites will have a country code at the end of the address (e.g. .uk for the United Kingdom or .ca for Canada).

The URL extension can give you an idea of the type of site you are entering. Commercial sites (.com) contain a lot of database materials but they are profit-based operations, so they will have subscriptions, memberships, advertising, etc.. as well as information. Just because it is a commercial site doesn't mean that it won't provide some great information for free—you just have to tolerate some advertising. Cyndi's List is a great example of a powerful, free genealogical site that just happens to be commercial.

The FamilyTreeMaker.com, Genealogy.com, and Ancestry.com Web sites can help you stay up-to-date on all the new books and products available to genealogists. While they do offer information for a fee, they also provide an immense amount of free education and information regarding genealogical services, products, and resources. **Many products for genealogists that pertain to general research and the Internet aren't usually available in local bookstores.** Keeping up with new products is easier on the Internet with the articles, advertising, reviews, etc. that are out there. Most companies that deal in genealogical books and information have Web sites listing their products. Search them out by looking at genealogical publications such as *Family Tree Magazine* <www.familytreemagazine.com>, *Everton's Family History Magazine, Family Chronicle Magazine* <www.familychronicle.com>, and *HeritageQuest* <www.heritagequest.com>, to name just a few.

Searching for genealogical supplies on Cyndi's List will present you with many options. These will almost always be commercial sites, but they will provide you with many additional contacts and suppliers. Advertisers

Reminder

generally list their URL, mailing address, and toll-free number in ads posted in genealogical publications and on other Web sites relative to the subject matter. Read the many advertisements and articles dealing with the Internet and you'll greatly expand your knowledge.

Genealogical publications dealing with the Internet, software, and databases include *Family Tree Magazine* <www.familytreemagazine.com> and *Family Chronicle Magazine* <www.familychronicle.com>. These publications and their Web sites review software, list many relevant Web sites, and contain information about genealogical happenings all over the U.S. and Canada. They also have wonderful articles on all types of records from all over the world. They are just two examples of what is available for today's researchers.

Sites with extensions such as .org, .edu, and .gov will provide a wide range of data and information—most of it for free. Sites bearing the .org extension are nonprofit organizations, such as the FamilySearch Web site of the Mormon Church.

## THE BAD

Many researchers have little or no knowledge of how databases or electronic media are created. How the data is transferred from written to electronic form affects how you search the database. Understanding the different means of creating electronic databases will help you determine the most effective way to utilize the information included.

There are three basic methods used to create an electronic database.

1. Text based—The data from any written source is keyed or typed in manually, a process called data entry, which makes the database everyword searchable. This means that every word within the database can be searched for, not just key words.

2. Image based—The original text is scanned as an image rather than entered as text. The computer doesn't recognize words on the page and only sees a picture made up of thousands of tiny dots. This means that the search capabilities are limited and it's *not* every-word searchable. In scanned-text databases, the indexing properties are usually no better than the original book's index. What is indexed is up to the publisher of the database. Most books are scanned in this manner and are therefore not ideally suited to searching.

3. OCR—This means Optical Character Recognition. The text of a book is scanned as an image. The computer and accompanying software

then translates the individual pictures of letters into a text document. This should make the database every-word searchable like the data entry method. This, however, depends on the accuracy of the software. OCR software is far from reliable and there are often mistakes that go unnoticed by proofreaders.

**Important**

**If the original data wasn't in a typed format, you must also be concerned about the interpretation of the handwritten information.** How experienced is the person reading the document and typing it into a database? How clear and legible is the document they're working with? Is their work then proof-read before inclusion into the database?

These and so many more questions must be asked whenever you approach a new electronic or digital database. Since the computer is a literal machine, it will in most cases search for exactly what you ask it to without regard to other possible spellings, variations in names, abbreviations, etc. There are some databases that will include close matches, other possible spellings, etc. in the results they present, but they are few and far between.

The databases on the FamilySearch Web site produce the most variations to any given spelling. While some databases will allow a search using the Soundex Code (a code created to group like-sounding names together based on the consonants and their order in the name), they will not show results if the first letter of the name differs. This is especially important with names beginning with C, K, S, Z, J, G, and other consonants with multiple sounds. I once found the name Fopiano under the spelling Phopiano. This didn't show up in the Soundex search, as the code for Fopiano is F150 and the code for Phopiano is P150.

When using the Soundex search option, you must be sure that all variations of the surname are coded alike. Make a list of the variations in spelling that you have encountered, and code each variation individually to see if the code changes. Some examples of fairly simple names resulting in different codes are:

Rogers = R262          Waite = W300
Rodgers = R326         Weight = W230

Whenever I am searching for a new surname, I use the FamilySearch Web site to see what other spellings might show up. I did this when I was searching for a Mahon (M500) family. One of the options I had not considered was McMahon/MacMahon (M255). I have found this name recorded with and without the Mc/Mac prefix. Some of the family members kept the prefix while others dropped it.

---

**SOUNDEX CODING GUIDE**

| The number | Represents the letters |
|---|---|
| 1 | B P F V |
| 2 | C S K G J Q X Z |
| 3 | D T |
| 4 | L |
| 5 | M N |
| 6 | R |

Disregard and do not code the letters A, E, I, O, U, W, H, & Y

---

The Weight/Waite surname produced several alternate spellings that coded the same (Wacht, Wayte, Wate), and Wacht turned out to be the original spelling of the name in the immigrant generation. Knowing all possible spellings is especially important when looking in printed indexes and databases that don't allow the Soundex search option.

To determine which of the mentioned methods were used to create the database you are using, you'll need to do a few test searches. If the database contains names (as most of the ones genealogists use will), try a search using a common surname. I will often use "Smith" or "Jones" as my test name since they almost always occur in any given database. Enter "J Smith" in the search criteria. What results does the search provide? Do you only get those that are exactly as you typed it—J Smith? Do the results include all persons whose name begins with J and have Smith as the surname? These would include hits of James Smith, Jane Smith, Jas. Smith (with James abbreviated), J. P. Smith (middle initial included), or any name containing the Smith surname and a J in any other position. This one small test of the search capabilities tells you a lot about the database and how you need to use it. If the results presented to you only include the exact search criteria "J Smith" (without the period after the J), you'll have to do multiple searches under every possible spelling of the first name, along with searches including every middle initial and middle name—including "J. Smith" with the period. Doesn't sound so easy any more, does it?

You can take this test one step further by typing in "James Smith" as the criteria. Does the database show results for "James Smith" including middle initials? If results include James E. Smith, James D. Smith, etc., then the middle name or initial does not affect the search results provided. That actually makes it easier, since many times we have no idea if a person actually had or used a middle name or initial.

Look at the results from the James Smith search again. Are given names that have been abbreviated (such as Jas. or J.) included in the results? If not, you will need to familiarize yourself with all of the possible abbreviated forms of any given name. This also includes nicknames. James could be listed as Jim, Elizabeth as Eliza or Betty, and Margaret as Maggie, Peg, Peggy, or Marge. The possibilities are almost endless.

**Tip**

**By doing several test searches you'll gain a better understanding of how to find your specific person.** Sometimes it is easier to include less specific criteria in the search. If the database provides results that include all of the first names beginning with or including the letter J, you don't need to do multiple searches for all the possible variants.

Take another look at the results provided for the J Smith search. Do all of the results include only the "Smith" spelling of the surname? Do variants such as Smyth or Smythe show up in the results? Regardless of how you think the family name is spelled, many census takers and others who recorded the name might have spelled it differently. There was no standard spelling of any kind before the early twentieth century and the institution of the Social Security system. Many clerks spelled names phonetically or the way they thought it should be spelled. Many individuals were illiterate and couldn't spell their own name or check the accuracy of what was recorded. This is especially true with immigrant names. These individuals couldn't read or write in their native tongue, let alone in English! This said, you must always keep an open mind and look for all possible spelling variations, no matter how bizarre!

Another test search to determine if the database is image-based or text-based is to search for a word or name that is most likely within the text. Think about the subject matter of the database or online book. Was the data previously published in book format? You should search for something that you think would appear or does appear in the book index. Once you get a result, find several other facts or details on the page that are not as specific as a name or that don't appear in the printed book index. I will usually pick a subject, place name, or other detail from the text. Now go back to the search screen and enter that subject, place name, or detail as the criteria for a search. Does the database come up with the same pages as it did the first time? Does it tell you that there are no matching entries? This might indicate that the indexing is minimal or that the database is constructed from images rather than text and is therefore not fully searchable.

Many databases available to today's researchers are previously published books, some with good indexes and others with almost useless ones. In the push to get as many resources online as possible, many previously published books—most no longer under copyright—were scanned or converted to text using OCR. Many of the census indexes currently available are digitized copies of the old AIS (Accelerated Indexing System) printed indexes. All of the inherent faults and problems that were in the original printed sources carry over into the digitized version. Slowly, new indexes are being created for those census years that previously were not indexed. Don't expect the ones with previously published indexes to be redone any time soon, however.

Another problem with data that comes from previously published or printed books is in knowing what books might be used to create any one database. Does the database information say which books were used to compile the data? Some CDs or online databases might list the books or publications used as source material somewhere in the information about the resource. Many have "How to use this database" or "More about this database" sections that most researchers never bother to read. It's important for you to know where the data came from. Were the books or records used to compile the database reliable? Were different versions of the book published? Later versions of books might include corrections of mistakes made in previous versions. These are important things to keep in mind whenever you use a computer source.

Once you determine what books or sources were used in the compilation, you have another problem at hand. When you find something in the database, does it indicate which of the multiple books or sources that specific record came from? If not, you will need to determine where the original record came from. Always keep in mind that published books of records are secondhand sources. Most of the pre-twentieth century records that family historians used were handwritten, so any typed versions are a secondary source at best. They may be several generations away from the original. All of the inherent problems that exist in reading and interpreting the documents are carried over into the digitized versions. You're still depending on one individual's interpretation of the original handwritten record. That interpretation may or may not be accurate. If you show several

**For More Info**

See *A Practical Guide to the "Misteaks" Made in Census Indexes*, edited by Richard H. Saldana.

different individuals a line in the census records and ask them what it says, you may get two or three different interpretations.

## THE UGLY

Now that I have rained on your parade and made you rethink computerized resources, I will finish the job by pointing out some downright ugly problems with online databases.

Sometimes you can do everything correctly and still not find your relatives. Don't give up—they may be in the database no matter what the search results say. Due to spelling errors, misinterpreted handwriting, unfamiliar names, or many other factors, they may not show up in any of your searches.

For example, I found one of my families in the 1850 Vermont census and printed a copy of the record at the local National Archives facility. Upon arriving home, I realized I could not read the page number on the record due to a dark copy. I went online to Ancestry.com's Web site to look up the entry. When you find an individual in the database, it lists the page number. This seemed like it would be a simple process, but it turned into a weeklong project!

I searched for my subject by name (copied directly from the census page) along with the county and town name. The database stated that there was no matching entry. How could that be? I had the census page right in front of me. I thought that perhaps the given name was interpreted incorrectly—it was an uncommon one (Linus Rounds). I eliminated the first name in the search criteria and still no results were presented. With the Round/Rounds surname being a common one in Addison County, Vermont, in 1850, I knew something was wrong. I then eliminated the name all together leaving only Addison County and the town of Starksborough in the search criteria—still no luck and no results. I continued to eliminate data fields until I was only searching for people (unspecified surname) in Addison County, Vermont. I was presented with many results, including my Linus Rounds in Starksborough. What went wrong? Upon closer inspection I realized that whomever entered the information into the database had listed the town name as St. Arksborough! The computer doesn't know that St. Arksborough and Starksborough are the same location. Nor will the computer recognize that Starksboro and Starksborough are two possible spellings for the same name.

Even worse, no matter how I entered the incorrect Starksborough name, with or without the period after the "St," I could not get the entry to come up. What if I hadn't already known that Linus Rounds was living in Starksborough in 1850? I would have made an assumption that he was living somewhere else and would have wasted many research hours looking for him. The poor guy was right where he was supposed to be all the time! The defect in the database kept him hidden.

I tried other searches for towns with names beginning with the letters "St" and found that the entire Vermont index had the same problem. Stowe was St. Owe, Stamford was St. Amford, etc. Now I was on a roll. I checked the other New England states. With the exception of Connecticut, every state east of the Mississippi had the same error in the database (I gave up at the Mississippi River). The only town in Vermont not listed this way was St. Johnsbury—it was listed as Saint Johnsbury—exactly as it was written on the top of each census page!

After nearly five years of reporting this major error to the people at Ancestry.com, it has finally been corrected. I haven't yet checked to see if every state was updated or just Vermont. While many errors do occur—and they are corrected eventually—always keep in mind that just because you don't find a person in the index, it doesn't mean they're not there. **It means that they are not there the way you are searching for them**. Remember—the computer is a literal machine and cannot think for itself. It does only what you tell it to do, not what you want it to do!

**Important**

Another problem with town names in several census indexes is in the misinterpretation of the handwritten town or locality name. I have seen Malone, New York, listed as Molone, Mulone, and Mulane in different databases. Again, bad handwriting and poor copies are probably the culprits. Remember to start with specific criteria. If you do not find anything, eliminate one data field at a time. Start eliminating fields with the most specific criteria (given name, then surname, then town, and finally county) until you are assured that it is not a typographical error causing the problem. There is a chance that they just aren't in the index! I managed to find the Malone entry by searching only the year of the census and the county. I then looked at the towns that showed up and realized the spelling error.

Another precaution for working with online databases is determining who submitted the information. This is especially true of databases that include family pedigrees. These include the *Ancestry World Trees* <www.ancestry.com>, *Ancestral File* <www.familysearch.org>, *World Family Tree* <www.genealogy.com>, and Web sites created by family researchers. Be wary when using the information from these databases. Most will not provide you with their sources. You may be able to contact the individual

---

### TIPS FOR USING ELECTRONIC RESOURCES

- Check the information for sources of the data. Many contain information from previously published books and sources.

- Verify the original source! Just because the information came from a computer does not make it correct! The data included is only as good as the original source and/or the transcriber's accuracy. Unless it includes original document images (such as microfilmed records), it is NOT a primary source.

- Keep in mind that many census indexes are based on the previously published index books. All the inherent pitfalls of the published books have carried over onto the CDs and databases.

- Some CD-ROMs and databases are text-based and others are image-based.

- The Internet and CD-ROMs are wonderful tools for those without easy access to the original books or records, but they are not a replacement for research of original and primary sources.

---

who posted the information, providing their e-mail address is supplied and is still current. I haven't had much luck when I contact individuals and ask them where they got the data they posted. Most can't tell me where it came from. Due to this lack of proven sources, you will want to use these sources as clues only and try to prove the validity of the information through more reliable means, preferably original records. I have solved many problems and leaped over some brick walls with information provided in these databases, but always be wary of unproven data. We'll cover your responsibility when posting data on the Internet in chapter ten.

Additionally, there are many CD-ROMs (by Family Tree Maker and other publishers) and online databases that are compiled family pedigrees from many sources. The majority of these won't bear any documentation and should be used with caution. Most are submitted by family researchers who may or may not have done the research themselves.

FIVE

# Truth or Fiction

Now that you've accumulated a lot of facts, stories, and family documents, you're ready to verify or debunk your information. If you want an accurate record of your ancestry, you must prove each fact and work from the present backwards, from the known to the unknown. If you take the information on just one record as fact, you might follow an incorrect family when researching. Just because a person has the same name as the ancestor you are looking for doesn't make him the correct individual. Do not start from a person generations ago and follow the lines down to the present. It's nearly impossible to research this way. Many researchers want to prove their descent from some famous or infamous historical person. They try to begin with that person and work forward. Trust me—it won't work!

When your ancestry is laid out for ten generations, there are 512 couples that are directly responsible for your existence. If any one of these 1,024 individuals had not lived, you would not be here! Pretty amazing. This applies to everyone, not just those with large families.

## TRUTH OR FICTION?

Most family stories have some truth to them but are rarely corroborated with documentation. It's your job as the family historian to determine the validity of all the information you have found. Pay close attention to the information as you record it on forms. Do the dates make sense? Does the chronology make sense? Many of today's computer programs that record your family tree have reports that indicate possible problems with the data.

**For More Info**

**FAMOUS FAMILY?**

*Finding Your Famous and Infamous Ancestors: Uncover the Celebrities, Rogues, and Royals in Your Family Tree,* by Rhonda R. McClure (Cincinnati: Betterway Books, 2003).

I had one birth that I entered that would have made the mother seventy-five years old at the time of her child's birth. This mistake would not be evident until it is put in context with her birth and marriage dates and ages. Be on the lookout for these discrepancies.

Divide the information into several categories. These categories might include vital records, family papers and stories, family Bibles, personal knowledge, or government records (censuses, tax lists, etc.). Which bits of information can be verified and how?

## VITAL RECORDS

Vital records are primarily birth, marriage, and death records for certain time periods. They may also include baptisms, divorces, adoptions, etc., or any fact that is or should be legally recorded or verifiable with official records. This of course will depend on when and where the event took place. **Many new researchers are surprised to learn that vital records were not always required or kept in the same format or locations as they are today.** It's important that you know the geographic location and understand the laws that governed the keeping of records in the time period you are researching. Many of the U.S. states did not require the registering of births, marriages, or deaths locally or statewide until the late 1800s or even well into the 1900s. There are many resources to determine when it was legally necessary to record these events in any specific locality.

It is crucial that you fully understand the complexity of the records you'll be using. Reading books or articles about a specific record type and the locality will enable you to have a realistic view of its relevance and accuracy. Knowing when the records were required by law doesn't always mean that the law was adhered to. Many states passed such laws and they were generally ignored for many years. Without enforcement, there was no motivation for the laws to be followed.

You also need to know what was required to be included in that specific record. Each state made their own rules and regulations that will affect the quality and quantity of information contained in any given record. Many researchers assume that the records will be as inclusive as they are today. Seasoned researchers know that just finding a record can sometimes be a bonus—if it contains all the information you're searching for, it's a miracle.

Most New England states did an admirable job of recording vital statistics from the very beginning (starting in the early- to mid-1600s). The further west you research, the sparser the records are. As individuals migrated west

**Important**

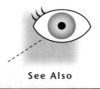

**See Also**

*The Genealogist's Companion and Source Book*, 2d Edition, by Emily Anne Croom (Cincinnati: Betterway Books, 2003)

through unsettled territory, there was no place to even register such events with the exception of the family Bible or other family papers. This can make your research difficult at best. I always wondered why some families seemed to have so many family papers and Bibles while mine had none. My mother's ancestors settled in New England in the 1630s and mostly stayed within the six New England states. Perhaps they didn't feel the need to keep detailed family records or Bibles because the records were being recorded in the towns they lived in. Families who were constantly on the move had no governmental authority recording the important events of their lives.

Determine where the record might be. Did the state the family resided in file the records at the town or county level? You'll find records at almost every governmental division within any given state. For instance, in New England vital records are recorded at the town level. Some states keep them at the town or county level, sometimes even subdivisions within the counties. The possibilities are almost as diverse as the states themselves. This is why knowledge of the locality and its laws governing such records is imperative. *Research the record before you use the record to research*!

There are many books and Web sites available to current family historians that make this task much easier than it was even ten years ago. Many of the Web sites popular with genealogists offer articles and valuable information pertaining to almost any type of record you may encounter.

Utilize these free resources and learn everything you can about the records and the locality you are interested in. I often print these articles out and read them later. This enables me to highlight important facts or things I might need to read more about.

In addition to determining if the record exists, knowing what will and will not be included in it will save you many disappointments. **By understanding the governmental purpose for the record, you'll better understand why specific information is or isn't there.** One of the most used records is the census. These were created as a means for the government to allot seats in the House of Representatives. Because of this, the names and correct spellings of each person's name were not crucial to the document. The government needed to know how many individuals were of legal age and able to vote. For many of the earliest census records (1790 through 1840), the only name they asked for was the head of the household. All others were simply listed in age and sex categories. Frustrating for the researcher, but perfectly sufficient for the government's needs. Each subsequent census

**For More Info**

*The Source: A Guidebook of American Genealogy,* by Loretto Dennis Szucs and Sandra Hargreaves Luebking, eds. (Salt Lake City: Ancestry, Inc. 1997)

**Notes**

year additional or different questions were asked, depending on what statistics the government was looking for.

So many researchers look for their immigrant ancestor's passenger record for years, only to find that it doesn't include the person's parents' names or even the individual's place of birth. Consider the original purpose of the record. Knowledge is a powerful time- and energy-saver. These records were created to serve a governmental need, and not for researchers seeking the details of their ancestors' lives. (See chapter four for record types.)

One of the most consistent problems that researchers face is inaccurate birth or marriage dates. Illegitimate births, marriages too close to a child's birth date, and other skeletons can be hard to deal with. Keep this in mind, especially when interviewing older individuals. Keeping an open mind and not taking these human mistakes personally will go a long way in making you a better researcher.

Many older individuals are secretive about family skeletons. They were raised in an era where you didn't discuss such things. Many individuals carried the stigma of their illegitimate birth their entire lives. I once found a record for a woman who died in Scotland in the late 1800s that stated the eighty-seven-year-old woman was "the illegitimate daughter" of John Russell and Mary Stewart.

## VERIFYING INFORMATION

Has the record you need survived to this day? Fires, natural disasters, or just plain neglect have caused records to be destroyed or simply lost over the generations. Most family historians don't want to find out that the evidence they need to verify their facts may not exist. However, it can be a good thing. Persistence is an important quality in today's researcher. We have all been told at one time or another that records were lost in a fire, only to determine later that they do exist. Sometimes this happens because the clerks responsible for their care do not know where those records are, or have been told by someone else that they burned. Records have been moved, stored, and otherwise shuffled around for centuries, and most of today's municipal workers do not deal with noncurrent records often enough to know their whereabouts.

This said, how can you determine if the record exists and where it might now be stored? You must find out which governmental agency or religious group would have created the original record or document. If the record was created at the town level, you should check the local library, town hall, historical society, and the Family History Library Catalog for copies. If the record was created at the county level, you should check the county courthouse, county clerk's office, state library or archives, and the Family History Library Catalog.

Many church records are no longer held in the local parishes or churches where they were created. They may be deposited in a church archive or in the parent church. This can prove to be a unique challenge—before you can verify your facts, you must determine that the record was actually created, that it still exists, and where you can see it.

Also, not all records in every state or country are public. You may not be able to gain access to more recent records (less than one hundred years old) if state laws prohibit it. If this is the case, you need to be creative in using other records to help you validate the information. **Again, understanding the record type and the laws governing it will save you much frustration and time.**

**Important**

## WEB SITES FOR VITAL RECORDS INFORMATION

Cyndi's List <www.CyndisList.com>—enter "vital records" in search box

World Vital Records <www.worldvitalrecords.com>—click on the state or foreign country you're researching in (not all are included)

Online Vital Records <www.onlinevitalrecords.com>—click on the locality of your interest

About Genealogy <http://genealogy.about.com>—click on "U.S. vital records"

Utilize the many books and Web sites that list laws governing access to any particular record. State or local genealogical societies in the area where you are researching can be your best allies. They will know what can and cannot be accessed, where to get the record, and what information will be included. This is especially important if you are researching in another country. The individuals who use the records every day both here and abroad can and will guide you with tips and advice that will be important to your success. They may also have better luck dealing with local clerks and record repositories, since they probably frequent the repositories and have no language or cultural barriers to overcome.

Another trait that will be helpful in your research is the ability to read between the lines. Many times a record contains the answer you are looking for, but it may not be obvious at first. Many people read a record for a

**For More Info**

One very good resource is Christine Crawford-Oppenheimer's book *Long-Distance Genealogy*. She offers many wonderful tips and advice on how to obtain records without traveling to distant locations.

specific reason and miss important clues buried in the text. One example of this is the following news article.

**Sotorno Montanari, Running for Shelter, Killed as Wife Looks On**
Running for shelter from the windstorm, Sotorno Montanari, 56 years old of 245 College Street was killed when a huge elm tree in Tyler Street near Eastern Avenue split in two, a falling limb crushing his skull. Death was almost instantaneous. Mrs. Montanari, looking on, helpless, from the window in the home of her sister, Mrs. A. Artioli of 126 Eastern Avenue saw her husband die.

Artioli escaped being struck by but a few seconds, an injury to his back, which prevented him from running, probably saved his life. He reached the house without knowing that his brother-in-law had been hit, declaring that sand in his eyes had prevented him from seeing the accident.

Dragged from beneath the debris Montanari was carried into the house still breathing. He died before medical aid could be summoned.

The men had been watching neighbors playing in a lawn bowling match. Seeing the storm approaching they decided to seek shelter. Halfway to the house, the elm tree crashed to earth, a 12-inch limb striking Montanari squarely on the head.

Montanari was employed as a sweeper by the Chapman Valve Company in Indian Orchard. He was a native of Bologna, Italy and had lived in Springfield nearly 13 years. Besides his wife he leaves two sons, Albert and John and a daughter, Mrs. Adella Balboni.

I had been searching for an obituary or death notice to confirm the family story that Saturno had died after being struck by lightning. The family story was almost accurate. A tree branch that had been struck by lightning hit and killed him.

## SQUEEZING OUT CLUES

This one news item contained enough information to keep my research going for some time. Any time you read a record you must ask yourself what can be inferred from the information it contains. The facts show that Saturno was fifty-six years old, married, an immigrant from Bologna, Italy, and lived on College Street in Springfield, Massachusetts. The information provided indirectly is just as important. Saturno's wife, whose given name is not mentioned, is a sister to Mrs. A. Artioli, who lived at 126 Eastern Avenue on 20 July 1926, the date of the article. I then used city directories to determine that the Artioli family was first recorded at that address in the 1914 directory. Some of the directories showed that Saturno's wife's name was Virginia. I now had addresses and dates to go with the names. The article also lists his surviving family members—more records to look for. By looking at the marriage and death records for the mentioned family members, I found the maiden name of Saturno's wife and her sister. The article states that Saturno had lived in Springfield for nearly thirteen years. This would put his immigration year at about 1913, if he came directly to Springfield. Further research then proved that he arrived in the United States on 13 March 1913. His age at the time of his death would place his birth about 1870. His subsequent birth record from Italy stated that he was born on 20 April 1870. Employment records for the Chapman Valve Company are another possible source of information. Almost all of the information provided by the news article matched the facts and information I already had, thereby giving credence to other undocumented family stories.

**In many cases an obituary or death notice, no matter how brief, may provide you with names, ages, surviving family members, a church affiliation, the undertaker who handled the body and funeral, and the cemetery where the deceased is buried.** You might also find a place of birth, parents' names, and names of organizations the individual belonged to. Every single piece of this information must be looked at. Squeeze every bit of information out of every source you encounter.

**Research Tip**

When looking at any record you should ask yourself the same questions a good journalist will ask: who, what, when, where, how, and why? But do not stop there. One friend refers to this as the "Doberman approach" to research. Once you get your hands on a record, don't let it go until you are certain you have utilized every possible fact and clue from it. Even the court system recognizes the preponderance of the evidence. When different events and records all fit together in a cohesive manner rather than contradict each other, you can come to a pretty reliable conclusion.

## INACCURATE INFORMATION

Another problem you may encounter is inaccurate information in a record. Just because you have a certified copy of, say, a birth record, doesn't mean that the information is perfect. In most cases, the information is only as accurate as the person who provided the information. We must always be on the lookout for possible mistakes or outright lies.

Some mistakes happen when the record is copied from the original, perhaps to a statewide index or onto an extraction form. Keep in mind that most clerks have a form onto which they will transcribe the data for the record you requested. These forms differ a great deal from one locale to another. Most of the original records are in large books containing many records on any given page. The clerks in most cases will not give you a photocopy, as it would include other records besides the one you want. They will usually type the information from the original onto their form. In some cases, there may be additional information on the original that is not asked for on the form and will therefore not be transcribed. Again, knowing what should be on any given record will help you evaluate these forms.

I once purchased a certified copy of a death record for Giuseppa Calabrese from a Massachusetts town clerk. The information did not seem to match the facts that I knew. The names of the deceased's parents weren't right and her age was off by more than ten years. Upon closer examination, I realized that the certified copy did not include the name of the person providing the information for the death record. The death occurred in 1911, and I wasn't sure if the record should have included this information. I called the clerk and had her check the original. Sure enough, the informant was listed (there was no space for the clerk to have typed this in on the form). She told me that the informant was the woman who ran the rooming house that Giuseppa lived in. Knowing this, I gave less weight to the certificate. I discounted most of the information the record contained. It would be unlikely that the informant would have known Giuseppa's correct age or her parents' names. Had the informant been a relative, or Giuseppa's husband, the information would carry more weight. The family historian must not only determine where to find a record, but also how much of it to believe. Sometimes simple mistakes can send you off in a totally wrong direction.

## TYPOGRAPHICAL ERRORS

One wrong turn involved a typographical error on a death certificate. The deceased died in the state of Maine. The death certificate listed her place of birth as Canton, Maine. Subsequent research could not place the family in Canton during the deceased's lifetime. A great deal of research went into trying to find the birth record or any record placing the family in Canton, Maine. The researcher then returned to the town of death and asked to look at the original record. Upon closer examination she realized that the place of birth was Canton, Massachusetts—not Maine. When the clerk was typing the document she inadvertently typed ME instead of MA. While there is a Canton in the state of Maine, that is not where the person was born. It was a very small mistake that wasted a lot of research time. Always keep in mind that the person typing the form might make such typing mistakes or just misinterpret the handwriting on the original. Most older records are handwritten and contain not only faded ink but bad penmanship as well.

This is especially true when looking for maiden names of women. **You must always evaluate the information by the relationship of the person giving it.** Would the person providing the information know the facts? For example, I will always put more weight on a marriage record than a death record. The people providing the information (the bride and groom) would know the facts better than another relative who might provide it on a death record.

**Important**

## DELIBERATE ERRORS

On more than one occasion I have found errors that can only be attributed to deliberate falsification of the facts. Since the individuals involved in any situation will be providing the information that goes onto a certificate, there is always a chance of falsification. Always ask yourself, when encountering information that doesn't seem to fit, if the information provided at the time of the event was accurate or deliberately deceitful.

One such instance occurred with a birth certificate for a man I was researching, Joseph Allen Robbins, supposedly born in 1910. His children had a certified birth certificate listing his date of birth as 8 October 1910. The birth certificate stated that his parents were Patrick Robbins and Mary Lewis. However, within the many family papers was Joseph's certificate of baptism, dated 10 October 1909. How could this be? At first I thought that perhaps there were two children born and given the same name, not an uncommon occurrence. The baptismal certificate listed only the sponsors' names, not the parents, so further research was needed to clarify the record. When a search was made of the birth records at the town level for October 1909, a birth was found listing the same given name, Joseph Allen, but a different surname. On this record, dated 8 October 1909, the parents were listed as Paul Burkhart and Mary Lewis. How could there be two birth certificates for the same individual listing two different fathers?

The town clerk was kind enough to do a little investigating and solved the puzzle. It seems that the birth actually was in 1909, along with the baptism. In October 1909, Mary Lewis was not as yet married to Patrick Robbins. The marriage took place in March of 1910. Apparently Joseph Robbins was always told, and had no reason not to believe, that he was born in 1910. When he went to register for the military his birth certificate couldn't be found in the 1910 listings. At that time his mother, Mary (Lewis) Robbins, went to the town hall and signed a sworn affidavit that he was born on 8 October 1910. In was not unusual in that time period for births to go unrecorded, because most births took place at home. It was up to the delivering physician, midwife, or family to register the birth.

Many such births were recorded later when it became apparent that the original had never been registered. This usually came to light when the individual needed a copy of his or her birth certificate to get social security benefits, go into the military, obtain a passport, or any other reason that identification or age would need to be verified. If the parents weren't living to sign an affidavit, other means, such as school records, were used to approximate the individual's age or date of birth. In this case, the information provided in the affidavit was intentionally falsified to hide the actual fact that Joseph was born before his mother married—and her husband was not his biological father. Had it not been for the baptismal certificate, this error would never have been known. Even the man's gravestone states his year of birth as 1910.

## LEGAL "LIES"

**Another circumstance in which the information might be incorrect is in the case of adoptions.** In every state, when an adoption becomes legal and final, a new certificate of birth is issued that lists the adoptive parents as the biological parents. This law makes it even harder to be sure that you've found the correct parents and corresponding medical history. Pay close attention to the date the information was recorded. Is the certificate dated near the birth or several years later? Is the name of the attending physician included? If there is a place for the physician's name on the certificate but it is blank, and if the recording took place several years or more after the birth, a red flag should go up. Again, knowing what should be included on the certificate and when it should have been registered will give you clues to its accuracy.

Another dilemma facing the researcher is a law in some states that required the husband of the mother to be listed as the father—even if the mother knew that the biological father was not her husband! I was amazed to learn that even today most states require the husband to be listed as the legally responsible individual for births by his wife.

I discovered this law when I was doing research for an adopted individual's birth parents. I located the birth certificate and recorded the parents' names. Further research located the birth mother. After speaking with her about the circumstances of the birth, she told me that she had provided the biological father's name to the hospital where the birth took place. She was told that if she was in a legal marriage her husband's name must go on the birth certificate. Her husband was in the military and had been overseas for nearly two years at the time of the birth, so there was no possible chance he was the child's father. The law required that his name be recorded on the certificate nonetheless. After checking with several other genealogists, I discovered that this was common.

## MISINTERPRETATION

Some records can be incorrect due to the transcriber misreading or misinterpreting the handwritten record. Most localities required birth, marriage, and death registrations long before state registration was required. When laws were subsequently passed that required towns and counties to register their vital records with the state, a variety of things occurred. In some states they were required to send copies of all previous records, as well as the new ones recorded. Other states only required the records to be sent from the date of the decision forward. As clerks went back through the record books and copied the information onto the state-required forms, many mistakes were made and some records were entirely missed.

I had looked for some time for my father's birth record in Massachusetts, to no avail. I tried every possible spelling that I could think of but had no luck. I asked myself how else I might be able to find the birth record. Alphabetical indexes were of no use to me. A visit to the town of his birth was my answer. Perhaps I could look at the original book, which should be in chronological order. The clerk I asked refused to let me look at the book. I had to ask for a specific record to obtain it. Frustrated, I went across the street to the local library to see what I might find.

In the state of Massachusetts, there are books referred to as "town reports." These books exist for towns with populations under ten thousand inhabitants. Towns of this size are governed by town meetings. All financial and political decisions and budgets are published yearly for all to see. For many years the town reports also included births, marriages, deaths, and burials that occurred in the town for that given year. The burial lists include deaths of citizens that took place in town, but also in other locations. The library had the books for the years 1900 through 1930 in their reference room. I looked in the books for the year 1912, when my father was born. Sure enough, his birth was there. It was, however, listed incorrectly. His father's given name, Bruno, was listed as the surname and his surname, Gannizzi, was listed as his given name. Add to this the fact that the surname was actually Iannizzi and you can see how many mistakes were made on just one record! I made a trip back across the street and asked for the birth on 24 August 1912 for Joseph Bruno. I pointed the mistake out to the clerk and she looked carefully at the book. The clerk who had originally recorded the birth had written the entry as *Gannizzi Bruno*, with no comma placed between the surname and given name. The clerk who then transcribed the record for inclusion in the town report and statewide index misinterpreted the original. The handwriting clearly (at least to me) spelled Iannizzi, but the clerk, unfamiliar with the old script, read the first letter as a "G" rather than an "I." Either way, the record wasn't listed in the index where it should have been. Be persistent and creative when looking for records!

**Reminder**

**All in all, you must always be skeptical of any unverified information.** Just because you have a certified record doesn't make it an accurate one. Many researchers put far too much confidence into the "official" record. You must ask yourself if there is a possibility the record is incorrect. If anything in or about the record doesn't look or feel right, you must look further. As you can see, there are many reasons a record might be wrong.

Now that you have the daunting task of verifying everything, we can move on to the records themselves.

SIX

# Where Are the Records?

O nce you have constructed your basic pedigree chart and reviewed what you already have, you'll need to access many types of records to fill out your family tree. As we saw in the last chapter, there are many forces working against you. Missing records, deliberate falsifications, fires, floods, careless transcriptions, and misplaced records, while frustrating, can make you a better researcher. I consider myself a detective in many ways. Learn to look at every scrap of information, figure out how to verify it, and then determine which record best suits that goal.

Before you begin your search in records, determine what records exist for the geographic area as well as the time period in question. An excellent source is the USGenWeb <www.usgenweb.org>. There is one Web site for every county in the United States. Using these sites before you jump into research will give you a better understanding of what you are going to encounter. It might also provide you with resources that you had not previously considered. Knowing what a record holds and where you can easily access it is important information.

The records that you will use in the beginning are fairly basic ones—the ones researchers come back to over and over again. Thankfully, in most cases most of these are fairly accessible. With the exception of vital records in some states, the other records covered in this chapter are readily available. Some may require you to order microfilm, visit a library or courthouse, or perhaps write a few letters. See *Long-Distance Genealogy* by Christine Crawford-Oppenheimer and my book, *The Weekend Genealogist*, for ideas and strategies for today's time-starved researcher.

**Notes**

**For More Info**

For locations and holdings of regional NARA facilities, see <www.archives.gov/fac ilities>.

**While varied records are held at state, county, and local levels, there are specific facilities that also hold these records.** Determining the correct facility for your research interests and specific records is crucial.

## RESEARCH FACILITIES
### National Archives and Records Administration (NARA)

The NARA facility in Washington, DC, along with the thirteen regional facilities located around the United States, houses an almost endless supply of records for the family historian. Their most popular records are the United States federal census enumerations. The enumerations (listings of residents) currently available cover the time period from 1790 through 1930. The 1940 enumeration will be released in the year 2012, when the seventy-two-year privacy period has expired.

**Other Popular Records Held by NARA Include:**

- Passenger lists for immigrants arriving in the country
- World War I and II draft registration records
- Civil War pension indexes (original pension files are in Washington, DC, only)
- Revolutionary War pensions and records of service
- Naturalization papers (only those for the courts in their geographic coverage area)
- Records of postmasters and lighthouse keepers
- Agricultural and manufacturing enumerations
- Slave and Native American records

Note that not all of these records are held in all NARA facilities. For a complete list of facilities and records see the third edition of the *Guide To Genealogical Research in the National Archives of the United States* or visit <www.nara.gov> and click on "Research Room" then "Locations and Hours."

**Important**

NARA facilities do not have birth, marriage, or death records for individuals unless the event took place on a military base overseas. Vital records are almost always state, not federal, records.

### National Libraries

The only national library in the United States is the Library of Congress, located in Washington, DC. This library is worth a visit by every researcher at least once in their lives. All family genealogies and books that have been copyrighted will be held in this facility. In addition to these family histories there is an immense collection of maps, photos, and federal, state, and local histories. The holdings are almost limitless. Every time I visit I find more records to use, and I doubt I'll ever exhaust the resources held there.

Some of their collections are available online, as is the card catalog. I have used the photographic collections extensively. Visit the Web site <www.loc.g ov> to access the card catalog and some of the collections. Click on "Index A-Z" to see an alphabetical index of the collection. Clicking on "G" then on "Reference Guides for Genealogical Research" will take you to a listing that includes the genealogy resources. There are resource guides and an extensive "Before You Begin" section that you should read. It explains what is available at the library through a loan and purchase program and its photoduplication services. You will find maps, photographs, and articles on everything from baseball to railroads. You can also hear sound recordings from many cultures and eras in history. Quite amazing!

## State Libraries and Archives

Every state in the country has a state library, archives, or both. **Most facilities have an active Web site that lists the location, hours, holdings, and information regarding access to the records.** State libraries and archives will house a variety of records. These might include vital records (births, marriages, and deaths), census records (population, agricultural, and manufacturing schedules), newspapers, city directories, historical information, military and regimental histories, biographies, and published family histories.

Each state library or archive might hold some, but not necessarily all, of these records. Invest some time researching the state facility and its collections, and you will be provided with almost endless research possibilities.

Under the United States Newspaper Program, there is one library (usually the state library or archives) designated as the repository for all copies of surviving newspapers relating to that state. In some cases it may be a large public library, as in Massachusetts, where the Boston Public Library houses the collection. Many of these microfilmed newspapers can be borrowed on interlibrary loan from the holding facility for use in your local library. It is a wonderful way to access newspapers from all over the United States.

### State Libraries and Archives Might Hold

- Census records
- State and county histories
- Maps from different time periods
- Land records (both local and state records)

**Internet Source**

See <www.usgenweb.org> or <www.cyndislist.com> to find Web sites for state archives and libraries. Books such as *Ancestry's Red Book*, *The Source*, the *Family Tree Resource Book for Genealogists* and many how-to books will also list these facilities.

- Records pertaining to wills and probates
- Newspapers for the state
- Vital records (especially from early periods)
- Cemetery data (locations or transcriptions)
- Military history

## County, Local, and University Libraries

Private, educational, and free public libraries exist all over the country. Depending on the state you are researching, there may only be free public libraries at the county level, while in other areas they're located in towns. The collections they house vary greatly. County libraries tend to have collections of broader scope than town libraries, since the geographic area they cover is larger. Many county and local libraries have history or genealogy rooms devoted to those types of records. You need to determine what records and special collections they might house that would aid in your research. Always look for local-interest collections, manuscripts (one-of-a-kind records), local newspapers, family files, and local family information. Many times, as in New England, there might be several town libraries within one county that have extensive genealogical and historical collections.

Use USGenWeb <www.usgenweb.org> to find county, local, and educational libraries. Links may be provided to online catalogs listing their collections. Some collections themselves may even be accessible via the Internet. Check to see what collections might be duplicated in the state library or archives. If the records you need are in both locations, perhaps the larger facility will house additional records of interest.

Educational libraries associated with state or private colleges and universities house wonderful historical collections. In addition, they have many sources for social history of the geographic area. These facilities also often have extended hours to accommodate student schedules. I have located many state and local histories, military records, and newspapers in such facilities. Most have their card catalog available online to make it easier to determine ahead of time what they might have.

Libraries noted for their large genealogical collections include the Allen County Public Library in Fort Wayne, Indiana; the New England Historic Genealogical Society library in Boston, Massachusetts (a private library that requires membership or a fee for nonmembers to use); the Newberry Library in Chicago, Illinois; and the Daughters of the American Revolution Library (DAR) and the Library of Congress in Washington, DC.

**County, Local, and Educational Libraries Might Hold**

- Census records
- State, county, and town histories
- Social histories
- Local land records
- Maps showing local landowners
- Newspapers for the area
- Vital records (especially from early periods)
- Cemetery data (locations or transcriptions)
- Military history
- Family files or lineage papers containing previous research

## Historical and Genealogical Societies

Most states have historical and genealogical societies on the state, county, and local levels. At times these societies serve together as one entity, but many are separate groups. Over the years these separate organizations have begun interacting more than ever, providing both historical and genealogical information to researchers. Since the history of an area has such an impact on its population, family history cannot be done effectively without historical information, and vice versa.

**Historical societies often hold wonderful photographic collections pertaining to their local areas and citizens.** These might include class photos, yearbooks, lists of residents who served in the military, photos of buildings, or maps showing land owners. They might also have photos from local organizations, both social and fraternal, as well as extensive records on some families.

Hidden Treasures

Genealogical societies, whether state, local, or ethnic, contain some real jewels for the researcher. Many individuals who have done extensive research on families have deposited copies of their work in these facilities. Some societies might have lineage papers filed by others in order to join the group. Such organizations include the Daughters of the American Revolution (DAR), Grand Army of the Republic (GAR), Mayflower Society, Descendants of the Founders of Ancient Windsor (CT), etc. Many states also have pioneer societies or organizations that document the early settlers in the area. These can provide you with valuable information. DAR has a large collection of Bible transcriptions that have been made available in libraries across the country. Local societies may have additional Bible records donated to their society.

### Historical and Genealogical Societies Might Hold

- Photo collections
- Lineage papers, Bible records, or family files
- Maps of early settlements
- Class photos or yearbooks
- Ledger books from early local businesses
- Cemetery records
- Church and local histories

## Family History Library and Local Family History Centers

This library holds the largest collection of worldwide genealogical records anywhere on earth. For many years the Family History Library (FHL) in Salt Lake City, Utah, has been microfilming records all over the globe to preserve them. These records are so numerous and extensive that trying to list them all would be impossible. (See *Your Guide to the Family History Library* by Paula Stuart Warren and James W. Warren for more in-depth coverage of this library.) The wonderful thing about this library and its holdings is that the records may be used at any of the over three thousand Family History Centers (FHC) around the world. Nearly all of the microfilmed records (with some exclusions) can be rented for a nominal fee for use at any local FHC.

Today's researcher has records available to him that previous generations had to travel around the world to obtain. Some of the records were microfilmed before World War II and some records exist today only in the microfilms of the FHL, having been lost or destroyed through war, fire, or other disasters.

The only items in the Salt Lake City collections that do not circulate are books. Many of the books have been microfilmed and the film copies can be borrowed, but the original books remain in the FHL facility. Many of the records available through NARA and state, county, and local libraries and archives are also available through the FHL and the local FHC. If access to the original records is impossible for you, perhaps due to great distances, the FHL catalog may provide you with a local option.

To determine where the local FHC might be in your area, visit the Web site at <www.familysearch.org> and click on "Find a Family History Center near you." After entering a country, state, and town, you will see a list of the FHCs in your area. Each center is shown with its location, telephone number, and hours of operation. Remember if you live near a state border, also enter the other state—the closest center may be there. Since all FHCs are staffed by volunteers, you should always call and verify the hours of operation. The staff are invariably helpful but not necessarily knowledgeable in specific research areas. They can provide you with research guides (also available online) to specific geographic areas or record types. Most centers have Internet access to the Salt Lake City facility, the library catalog, and the extensive resource guides, word lists, and other research helps. Getting to know this library and its holdings is a must for every researcher.

Some records can be accessed via the Web site, including the International Genealogical Index (IGI) and Ancestral File (linked pedigrees submitted by individuals), census records (transcribed copies of the 1880 United States census and the 1881 British and Canadian census), the Social Security Death Index, and so much more.

## BOOKS AND MAGAZINES

**Perhaps the most valuable tool for learning about records, their use, and where to locate them are books and periodicals.** The sheer number of books currently available is amazing. Ten to fifteen years ago there were only a few reference books available. Today entire books are dedicated to a single record type, facility, or country. Learning what books are available, locating these books, and accessing them takes a little time. Bookstores often do not have good selections of genealogical books or magazines.

**Printed Source**

The number of genealogical magazines available, either by subscription or on the newsstand, has also grown in recent years. By obtaining these publications, you can keep up-to-date on all of the new books, records, and Web sites currently available. Some of the more popular magazines are *Family Tree Magazine* <www.familytreemagazine.com>, *Family Chronicle* <www.familychronicle.com>, *Ancestry Magazine* <www.ancestry.com>, and *Everton's Family History Magazine* <www.everton.com>. These publications have informative articles on all types of records and research strategies, as well as reviews of Web sites, software, and published books. Keeping up on all of the new books, software, and Web sites is easier when you subscribe to such publications. Many book publishers also advertise in these publications and maintain Web sites listing available books.

Another way to learn about new or helpful books is to visit the Web sites in specific states and counties <www.USGenWeb.org>. Many of these sites list books that are locally published or books that volunteers will do free look-ups in. Since many societies around the country publish books locally, you may never realize that these resources exist any other way.

For specific research subjects, you can use one of the major bookseller Web sites such as Amazon <www.Amazon.com> or Barnes and Noble <www.barnesandnoble.com>. These sites allow you to search by subject (searching for "genealogy," for example, will present you with over twenty thousand titles), author, or title. This is a great resource that you can access right from your home computer. Once you determine what books exist that might be of interest, you can purchase them online, order them at any local bookstore, or try to locate a copy in a library or through the interlibrary loan program.

The sheer number of facilities and records available to today's researcher is almost endless. New books, articles, and even library collections are more available today than ever before. The advent of computers and the Internet, along with digital technology, is making online access to actual records a reality within our lifetime. This is a wonderful time to be a family historian!

SEVEN

# Records Galore

A s outlined in chapter six, resources can be almost endless if you keep an open mind. Almost anything can result in additional information. My mother kept a scrapbook during the time that my father was ill. She put all of the cards and letters he received into the scrapbook, which recently surfaced in a box of old photo albums. Reading through all of the cards and letters, some signed "your cousin" or "your aunt," opened up new avenues for research. How were these previously unknown people related? Wonderful new information has surfaced due to this unusual source.

My grandmother, who died in 1973, used Mass cards (cards typically given to those attending a Catholic funeral) for bookmarks. Mass cards usually have a prayer printed on one side with the name of the deceased and the death date. The front of the card will typically have a picture of a saint or other symbols of the church. As her daughter slowly cleaned out and disposed of a lot of books, she always saved these cards for me. Some of the individuals named on the cards were unknown even to her. Since all had names and death dates, I was able to look up the death records and have added several people to our family tree.

**While you should never stop looking for home sources, you will need to look outside your family for additional information.** Once you get beyond the knowledge of living family members, civil and historical records are next. Most people think historical records do not pertain to their family, but records created by government, the military, or individuals are all part of our cumulative history. Our ancestors weren't just statistical entities but living, breathing members of society. As such they left records and clues behind—just waiting for us to find them!

Reminder

**Research Tip**

Census records can be found at all National Archives and Records Administration (NARA) facilities and the Family History Library (FHL) in Salt Lake City and its Family History Centers.

**For More Info**

**BOOKS TO DETERMINE BOUNDARIES**

See the *Map Guide to the U.S. Federal Censuses, 1790–1920* by William Dollarhide and William Thorndale (Baltimore: Genealogical Publishing Company, 2000) or *The Family Tree Resource Book for Genealogists,* Sharon DeBartolo Carmack and Erin Nevius, eds. (Cincinnati, Ohio: Family Tree Books, 2004) to learn about shifting boundaries.

# CENSUS RECORDS 1790–1930

Using the information you have compiled from family papers and stories, you will need to assess where to go next. There is no single answer to the next step. Do you have enough information to find your grandparents or great-grandparents in the 1930 United States census records? For most researchers, the United States decennial census (every ten years) is the place to begin. Kathleen W. Hinckley, author of *Your Guide to the Federal Census,* states "The U.S. federal census is the foundation of genealogical research." Hinckley's book is a wonderful resource for learning not only about the federal census but other census types as well, such as territorial, state, and military census records. Any listing of persons, businesses, or goods (manufactured or grown) is considered a census. While most researchers will use the population schedules (the lists of people), you will also want to consider using the agricultural and manufacturing schedules as you progress in your research. If your ancestor farmed or owned a factory or business, these schedules can give you a picture of his productivity and what and how much of any specific product was grown or manufactured. Again, learn about the record before you use it for research!

The most effective way to use census records is to create a timeline for a particular family or individual. Look at the birth and death years and decide what census records the person *should* appear in. Creating a timeline for your family can help you put them in historical perspective. What years were they living and where? Check to see if the town, county, or state lines changed over the period of your timeline, and look at the appropriate records.

Once you get into census records, you will be provided with enough clues to keep you busy for quite awhile. Always look at the most recent census available and work your way backward in time. Information gleaned from a more recent census can lead you back to a location for the previous census (e.g., where were all of the children of the couple born?).

Let's look at an example of how to determine which censuses to search. Hoxey Constant Rogers was born about 1840 in Vermont and died in 1929 in New Hampshire. I determined that the state and county borders didn't change during his lifetime and he should appear in at least seven census enumerations (1850, 1860, 1870, 1880, 1900, 1910, and 1920). If the individual served in the Civil War, which Hoxey Rogers did, or was otherwise considered a veteran he might appear in the 1890 Veteran's Schedule—making his total number of possible censuses eight.

Since the information provided in each enumeration differs, **it is best to look at every available census and compile an overview for the individual or family** (see Figure 7-1 on page 82). Always take into account the inaccuracies of census data. None of the information provided to the census taker had to be proven or even provided by the individual it pertained to. One person in the household, sometimes a child, provided the data. If the family was not at home, the census taker might obtain the information from a neighbor. The actual lists you see don't indicate who provided the information. Keep in mind the example given earlier of death certificates being inaccurate due to the informant.

Once you have compiled the overview, you have additional information to work with. Watch the ages and birthplaces listed in each census. Are they consistent? Does the individual's age change about ten years each time? You will be amazed at the variances. By having an overview, you can get a better average age and possible places of birth for family members. This is especially important if your research subject moved westward or simply didn't stay in one place. By always looking at the latest census records first (remember, genealogists work from the present backwards), you can extract many clues.

Look at the family in several of the records. Were the children all born in the same state? Did the family own or rent their home? If they rented rather than owned, they may be more mobile than landowners and may move from one town to another over their lifetime. With the many indexes available today, it is a little easier to locate these vagabond ancestors. Before the electronic age, researchers had to look at the available printed index for each state separately.

It is also important to look at all of the family members, not just your specific ancestor. Knowing the names of all the children and where they lived can be the clue to finding the parents when they "disappear" from the homestead. Most often they went to live with one of the children— perhaps traveling completely across the country!

While researching a Perkins family in Vermont, I discovered that the elderly parents, who should have appeared in the 1900 census, were not where I thought they would be. Further research did not provide a death or probate record for either of the couple in the state of Vermont. They had lived on, and owned, the same farm for their entire married lives. In 1900, one of the sons appears to own the farm and the parents are not living with him. A tour of the family cemetery did not produce a gravestone

## COMPLETED CENSUS FORM

Name: Rogers, Hoxey Constant   b 1842   place VT   m 1865   place VT   d 1929   place Troy, NH   s/o Joseph A. & Annie D. (BARBER) ROGERS  
ADOPTED BY

Name: Emery, Teresa Rebecca   b 1847   place VT   d 1924   place Troy, NH   d/o Ira & Rebecca (BROWN) STEARNS EMERY

| YEAR/ROLL # | INFORMATION FOUND | SEARCHED | FOUND IN |
|---|---|---|---|
| 1870<br>M593 roll #693 | Rogers, Hoxey C.; 28y; male; carpenter; b VT; 00 real estate value, personal estate value $150<br>Rogers, Teresia; 23y; female, housekeeper; b VT<br>Rogers, Iona J.; 3y; female; b VT<br>Rogers, Ulysses S. G.; 29y; male; b VT<br>Rogers, Arthur L.; 11/12y; male; b Michigan | Rutland Co., VT | Denver, Newago Co., Michigan, family #109/109<br>page 4 |
| 1880<br>T9 roll #349 | Rogers, Alfred H.; 26y; male, carpenter; b VT (Hoxey's younger brother)<br>Rogers, Hoxey; head; male; white; 38y; b VT; teamster; father born Vermont; mother born Vermont<br>Rogers, Teresia; wife; female; white; 33y; keeping house; born VT; father born unknown, mother born unknown<br>Rogers, Ulysses S. G.; son; male; white; 12y; laborer; born Michigan; father born VT; mother born VT<br>Rogers, Orrie A.; son; male; white; 10y; laborer; born Michigan; father born VT; mother born VT<br>Rogers, Rebecca T.; daughter; female; white; 7y; laborer; born NH; father born VT; mother born VT<br>Rogers, Helen K.; daughter; female; white; 5y; born NH; father born VT; mother born VT<br>Rogers, Euphannia; daughter; female; white; 4y; born VT; father born VT; mother born VT<br>Rogers, Hoxey E.; son; male; white; 2y; born NH; father born VT; mother born VT | Cheshire Co., VT<br><br>Westminster, Windham Co., Vermont | Cheshire Co., VT<br>page 4<br><br>Westminster, Windham Co., Vermont<br>#425/453 |
| 1890<br>Veterans Enumeration<br>M123 roll #40 | Rogers, Hoxey C.; Sgt.; Co. I; 2nd Vermont Volunteers; enlisted 20 June 1861; discharged 1 Dec 1863; service 2 yrs. 5 months & 11 days disability incurred—shot in right leg, comments—re-enlisted veteran | Rutland Co., VT<br>Windham Co., VT | |
| 1900<br>T623 roll #945 | Rogers, Hoxey C.; head; male; white; born Apr 1841 in VT; 59y; married 35yrs; farmer; father born VT; mother born VT; rents<br>Rogers, Teresia; wife; female; white; born Mar 1846 in VT; 54y; married 35 yrs; father born VT; mother born VT; mother of 15 children / 4 living<br>Rogers, Elliot; son; male; white; born Jul 1882 in VT; 17y; single; father born VT; mother born VT; farm labor<br>Rogers, Seneca; son; male; white; born Apr 1885 in NH; 15y; single; father born VT; mother born VT; attending school<br>Rogers, Mary A.; daughter; female; white; born June 1892 (?) in NH; father born VT; mother born VT; attending school | Hillsborough, Cheshire County, New Hampshire | ED #45; page 27 lines 86-90 |
| 1910<br>T624 roll #861 | Rogers, Hoxey C.; head; male; white; 69y; married 45yr; born VT; father born NH; mother born NH<br>Rogers, Teresa; wife; female; white; 64y; married 45y; mother of 15 children / 4 living; born VT; father born —; mother born —<br>Rogers, Alexander; son; male; white; 25y; single; born VT; father born VT; mother born VT; laborer; odd jobs<br>Rogers, Joseph; son; male; white; born VT; father born VT; mother born VT; telegrapher; RR station (Joseph is actually Seneca—called Joe his entire life) | Walpole, Cheshire Co., New Hampshire | ED #48, page 5A lines 1-4 |
| 1920<br>T625 roll #1006 | Rogers, Hoxey; head; rents; male; white; 77y; married; born VT; father born NH; mother born NH; no occupation listed<br>Rogers, Teressia R.; wife; female; white; 72y; married; born VT; father born VT; mother born VT; no occupation listed<br>Moran, Rebecca T.; daughter; female; white; 45y; widowed; born VT; father born VT; mother born VT; sewing machine operator in blanket mill<br>Moran, Archie R.; grandson; male; white; 20y; single; born NH; father born NH; mother born NH; teamster in box factory | Troy, Cheshire Co., New Hampshire | ED #2 lines 1-4<br>family #221/250 lines 37-40 |

**Figure 7-1**  
Completed census overview form for Hoxey and Teresa Rogers.

for either individual, though most of the other family members were accounted for. Where did they go?

In this case I had to look back at all the census records accumulated for the family, along with the other records I had. I then searched and located each of the four known sons in the 1900 census to determine if the parents were living with them. I had no luck, so I went on to the seven daughters, who were a little more difficult to find due to marriages and name changes. This is why it is so important to pay attention to all records pertaining to the family group. My previous research showed the married names of most of the daughters. I searched for each of these daughters. Thankfully the parents were living with one of the daughters whose husband's name I already knew. They were living in the state of California! That's about as far from Vermont as you can get. This daughter had married a sea captain from Boston and they had migrated west in the 1880s. Why the parents chose to live with her rather than a closer relative is still a mystery.

Subsequent research yielded death certificates and obituaries from California. This included a front-page article written when the mother died. The headline in the San Francisco newspaper read: *Mrs. E. A. Cootey, Who Died Leaving 108 Descendents—52 Grandchildren Mourn Her Death. Six Grandsons to Act as Pallbearers at Funeral of Aged Woman*. The article outlined the complete family history back nearly five generations, listing her parents, grandparents, all of her children and siblings, and even chronicled the military service for family members. Included in the information was Mrs. Cootey's maiden name as well as the maiden names of her mother and grandmother! It was certainly worth the effort to discover her whereabouts in the 1900 census. At the time of her death (10 July 1910), the article stated she had lived in California for twenty years.

When looking at any single census, be careful to extract every piece of information possible. Hinckley's book lists all of the questions the census taker asked and recorded for each census enumeration. **Knowing what every column stands for, including those where only checkmarks or hash marks are recorded, is crucial to your research.** Later census records (1900–1930) ask specifically if the person owns or rents his place of residence. Sometimes a question is asked in a roundabout fashion. Such is the case for land or home ownership. The early census records (1850–1870) do not ask the ownership question specifically but rather "What is the value of your real estate owned?" The column will either be blank (meaning no property owned) or have a dollar figure in it. If the column reads $1,000, then the individual

**Research Tip**

owns real estate valued at this amount. Again, the answer to the ownership question is there, just not in the direct form you might expect. If an individual owns property, you should look for land transfers or probate records disposing of the land after the person's death.

The first census to record individuals of foreign birth is the 1870 federal census. The enumerator listed the place of birth for each individual, but columns eleven and twelve asked if the father or mother of the individual were of foreign birth. In addition to this information, columns nineteen and twenty asked if the person was eligible to vote—perhaps a clue to the person's naturalization status.

In 1880 they asked for the specific place of birth for each enumerated individual and also that individual's parents. Look for clues as to where else the family or individual may have lived by looking at all family members, their corresponding places of birth, and the places of birth of their parents. Watch for discrepancies. If the mother of the household is listed as being born in Pennsylvania but the older children list their mother's birthplace as Massachusetts, it might indicate that the woman is not the mother of those children, but a second wife. All of these little details add up over the span of several census records.

Even though the federal census records are used by most family researchers at some time during their research, they are probably the most underutilized record when it comes to extracting all of the information provided.

## Other Census Records

### Population and Nonpopulation Schedules

The federal census enumerations include listings (schedules) for more than just the population. These various schedules cover the following:

- Agricultural products (what crops did your ancestor grow?)
- Defective, dependent, and delinquent classes
- Population schedules (some are listed under the state while others are under the territory)
- Products of industry or manufacturing (did your ancestor own a business?)
- Mortality schedules (lists of individuals who died in the previous twelve months)
- Social statistics
- Veterans (1890)

## CENSUS TERMINOLOGY

- *census*—an official counting and listing of persons or products for a specific timeframe and geographic area

- *enumeration*—the listing of persons or products recorded by a census taker

- *enumeration district (ED)*—the area or neighborhood assigned to a given census taker (enumerator)

- *enumerator*—the person assigned to compile a list of persons or products in any given census

- *population*—the people residing in a specific geographic area

- *schedule*—the form filled in by the census taker with answers to specific questions

- *Soundex*—a means of indexing surnames which groups like-sounding names together (by assigning a letter and number code to the consonants within the surname)

As discussed in chapter five, United States federal census enumerations (listings) were taken every ten years beginning in 1790 (1791 for Vermont). Some of these records have been lost over the years. Nearly the entire population schedule (the one listing individuals) for the 1890 census was destroyed by fire. A few pages survived the fire and water damage, but less than 1,000 names appear on those pages. An important portion that did survive was the veterans enumeration taken in 1890. This list included only those individuals who were veterans of the War of 1812 and the Civil War (Union) widows. They list only the soldier or widow and not the entire family. Only half of the veteran's census survived, from the state of Kentucky alphabetically through the states. For the states of Alabama through Kansas and part of Kentucky, the lists were lost or destroyed before the remaining schedules were transferred to the National Archives in the 1940s.

The veterans census lists can be important to your research: The census taker listed the soldier or widow's name (along with her late husband's name), his rank, regiment or vessel (for Navy veterans), his dates of enlistment and discharge, number of days of service, his current post office address, and the nature of his disability, if any. **Sometimes, when a widow was remarried, you might find her listed under her new surname with the name of her deceased veteran husband written above her name.** The enlistment dates

Important

and regiment he served in will lead you to possible pension and service records. Even if you know that your ancestor died before 1890, it is worth looking for his widow in the enumeration.

Population and mortality schedules also exist for slaves, Indians, and Indian reservations. Not all of these schedules were taken every ten years, but it is certainly worth looking for any additional schedules and the information they might provide.

## Using Census Records

Remember—before you use any record source, you should read articles or books relating to that specific record. You must understand what you are seeing in order to get the most from any single source. The federal census records are especially confusing to beginners and they miss many important clues. By understanding the questions that were asked in any given census year, you will know what to look for. I have encountered many researchers who have been compiling their family history for many years but completely overlooked information found in the census. Most people look at the names, ages, and perhaps occupations on any given census page. Yet in just the 1920 census alone there are twenty-eight columns of information. If you use only three to four columns of data, you lose about twenty-four other clues! Even the 1850 census (the first census to list all names within any given household) has thirteen columns. Using only three to four columns means that you have missed nearly 75 percent of the possible information!

Many microfilmed census records are difficult to read. These records were handled by hundreds of people before microfilming took place. This has resulted in dirty, faded, or water-stained pages. So reading the column headings can be difficult, if not impossible. Using extraction forms (printed forms that duplicate the census pages) or books on census records for reference will enable you to know what each and every column contains. Forms are available from many sources. (See chapter three for sources of forms.) While extraction forms are a great tool for knowing exactly what information the census includes, I do not use them for their intended purpose—extracting information. Let me explain my method.

If you transcribe the information from a microfilmed census page onto an extraction form, you've removed the family from its surroundings. There might be important clues in the neighboring households, the makeup of the neighborhood, or other family members living nearby. When you first begin using the census records, these clues may not jump out at you. Later, sometimes years later, you might look at the same census and notice other relatives living nearby that you didn't know about when you first saw the record. Having actual copies of the census records will enable you to review them whenever you find new family names or new information.

Another thing to remember is that when you transcribe information from one place to another, there's always a chance of error. This is especially true with census records. With the often poor quality of the image, wide pages with crowded lines of data, and old handwriting, it's easy to copy the incorrect line. The mistake researchers make most often is transcribing the line above or below the one they're interested in. You can avoid this by making a photocopy *first* and then transcribing the data onto forms. I lay the entire photocopied page out and highlight the lines I am interested in with a yellow highlighter. Then I can see the exact information I need to transcribe. I also don't want to waste time at the research facility copying information when I can do that at home. I save my time in any facility for research, not for processing the data. The cost of a print copy is cheap insurance that I will get all of the correct information from the record.

## STATE CENSUS RECORDS

Some states took additional censuses at times. These records can be especially helpful when they occur in the years between the federal enumerations. **Some of these have more detailed information on individuals that can be valuable.** The New York State censuses were taken in 1790, 1825, 1835, 1845, 1855, 1865, 1875, 1892, 1905, 1915, and 1925. The 1855, 1865, and 1875 census lists ask for the county of birth (if in New York), or the state or country of birth. The 1855 census asks how long they have been residents of the county they now live in. Even as early as 1845, New York asked if an individual was born in New York, New England, Latin America, British Empire, France, Germany, other European nations, or another state in the United States. The 1892 census is especially helpful due to the almost total loss by fire of the federal population census of 1890.

## VITAL RECORDS

If you've not traced your ancestors back to 1930 and so can't yet access the census records with family names and locations, you must do further research in vital records, church records, etc. Depending on the state that

**Notes**

**For More Info**

See *State Census Records* by Ann S. Lainhart for the existence and availability of these records.

your ancestors lived in, this can be a challenge. Some states consider their records to be public, while others have limited or no access to them. Most states, however, allow only family members to access some records. You will need to investigate the specific laws pertaining to your state of interest.

Determining the current laws governing the records in any state has become easier over the last ten years due to the Internet. Researchers can also download or print official request forms for copies of records. You can access these laws and forms using either Cyndi's List <www.cyndislist.com> (search for vital records) or USGenWeb <www.usgenweb.org> (go first to the specific state and then to vital records information). Remember that each state makes the laws governing their own records. Laws vary widely from state to state. Some states have published indexes to the records and these indexes may list the county or community that submitted the original record. You may then be able to obtain the record from local, rather than state, authorities. In most cases, the rules that govern access at the state level will be the same at the local level, but obtaining the record from the town or county may be faster. There are many reference books that list the laws governing access to vital records, but with laws constantly changing, Internet sources will probably have the most recent information while books may be out of date.

With rising identity theft, continuing budget cuts, and staff shortages, many states are now trying to pass new laws limiting access to these records. As a result, access rules may become more restrictive, or the records may be closed entirely over the next decade or so. This makes it even more crucial that you don't put this research off until you retire. Some states require letters of permission from the individuals the record pertains to or proof that you are a relative. In some cases you may have to produce a death certificate for the person in question to prove they are deceased in order to obtain the records.

Vital records, as we have already discussed, vary in completeness and accuracy in every period of American history. This holds true for vital records in foreign countries as well. Determining the availability of any specific record type in a given locale and time period is much easier today, however, than it was even ten years ago. When beginning to research in a new locale, learn everything you can about that area. When did the area achieve statehood? When was statewide registration of births, marriages, and deaths required?

As an example, let's say you need to verify a record from the town of

Lancaster, Worcester County, Massachusetts, for the year 1700. Lancaster was founded in 1653 but was part of Middlesex County until 1731, when Worcester County was created out of parts of Middlesex and Suffolk counties. The records kept by the town of Lancaster should still be in the town (Massachusetts keeps vital records at the town level), but all records kept at the county level (land, probate, court, etc.) for Lancaster are in Middlesex County (for the years prior to the formation of Worcester County). Where a town resides within the county system today is not necessarily where it has always been.

State registration, when available, makes it easier to locate records when a family moved around a lot. If you know only the state the person claims to have been born in and not the town, your search can be daunting. Utilizing statewide indexes can help you determine what specific town or county reported the record to the state level. While you can actually use the state copy of the record, keep in mind that it is not a primary source (an original record). Mistakes made when the records were copied, limited forms for recording the data, and other problems exist that may send you in the wrong direction.

When each individual state passed laws requiring state registration of all births, marriages, and deaths, a myriad of events took place. Many states, while technically having a law in place that required this registration, ignored the law. Because of this you may not find early state records to be complete. Some states required the clerks to go back through the old records and report all of them to the state. Some states created a form for the clerks to use that asked for only the most rudimentary information. Sometimes there is additional information in the original record that was not sent to the state. It also appears that in some states the clerks either intentionally or inadvertently didn't report all previous records. Making copies of these records (before photocopy machines) would have been a huge undertaking for any clerk. If you have looked at early records, scattered among the books of other business relating to the town, you can understand how difficult a task it was.

If the record you want isn't listed in the state index, look for other people with the same surnames you are researching. What towns or cities were they residing in? This can sometimes help you narrow down the scope of your research. Look for other surnames that tie into your family as well. Of course, this doesn't work if you are dealing with a common name. Sometimes you will feel that you are looking for a needle in a haystack.

Because genealogists work from the present backwards, you should already have some clues as to the birthplace of any individual. Does it appear on their death certificate or the certificates for any siblings? Perhaps the marriage record lists this information. Census records might provide a clue. Use all of these sources as a means to narrow your search area. You may have to look at the death and marriage records for all siblings of your ancestor to determine a location or perhaps a maiden name of their mother. This is another time when knowing everything you can about the family unit, rather than just your ancestor, comes in handy.

Some states were required to report births and deaths to the state much earlier than marriages. Determine when each of the record types was required, and by what governmental or religious authority, before looking for the actual record. Just because a law says that records were kept from 1830 on does not mean that the records are complete from that date forward—only that they were mandated. Texas, for example, required births and deaths to be reported to the state in 1903, but marriage records were not mandated until 1966.

## CITY DIRECTORIES

When you are researching more recent time periods, perhaps after the available census records, you will need to use other resources. **City directories, the predecessor to today's telephone books, can be a valuable resource.** This is especially true if your ancestor resided in an urban area. There are many different types of directories that get classified under the "city directory" heading. Some of these include voter registration lists and lists of homeowners or taxpayers. All of these can provide additional information to further your research. This type of record can place your research subject in a specific time and place. Because they are published annually or biannually, you can follow individuals between census enumerations. They are especially important after 1930, the time period when the census is not public.

Most city directories were published in the nineteenth and early twentieth centuries, and were published either annually or every other year. Some are suburban directories—they cover towns in the suburbs rather than the cities. In the suburban directories, there are often two or more towns within the same book. Most often you can find directories in local or state libraries, although town or county libraries might have some for their own area. Always keep a lookout for this type of book whenever you go to a library or archive.

Many city directories follow a similar format. The residents are listed alphabetically, followed by their occupation and employer, then their residential address. Most directories will use a cryptic form of shorthand and it is *imperative* that you understand all of the abbreviations used within the directory. Usually in the front of the book there is a list of the abbreviations and what they mean. Refer to it often to be sure you are correctly interpreting the information.

A typical directory entry might read:

**Balboni**  Achille grocer 970 Carew h do

Aldo rem to W. Spfd

Alessandro chauffeur 435 Dwight res W. Spfd

Angelina clk 302 Main bds 17 Whiting

Anthony (Balboni Bros) 6 Sanford bds 17 Whiting

Antonio h 468 Worthington

Bridget Mrs. h 190 William

Bros (Anthony and Louis Balboni) sign painters 6 Sanford

Caesar electrotyper PPubCo res W. Spfd

Charles emp 175 N Main h 17 Whiting

Leo emp BmfgA h 74 Hampshire Ind Orchard

Louis (Balboni Bros) 6 Sanford bds 17 Whiting

Mario h 749 Main

Olindo picture framer emp 392 Main res W Spfd

Sebastian confectionery and fruit 91 Bridge rms do

Teresa Mrs. bds 37 Ashmun

Vincent electrotyper PpubCo res W Spfd

This might look like code. All of the abbreviations refer to something. The most common are "bds" which means "boards"; "rms" mean they room; "h" means they have a house or are head of the household; "do" means ditto; "res" means resides; "rem" means removed. When someone is listed as "removed," it simply means they moved to the named city or state. This is helpful information when you lose people between census records.

For example, look at all of the individuals listed under the surname Balboni. Who is listed as living at the same address? In the example given, Angelina, Anthony, Charles, and Louis all live or board at 17 Whiting. This might indicate a familial relationship. Since the surnames are listed alphabetically, watch for other possible spellings. If one man is listed as "Bolboni" due to a misspelling, he will appear out of order and might be missed.

Another sample from the Springfield, Massachusetts, 1917 directory shows this problem.

**MONTANARI**
　　Cesare lab h 35 Hubbard av
　　Fortunato lab h 112 Greene
　　Joseph (Broadway Vulcanizing
　　　　Co.) 80 Bridge rms 112
　　　　Greene
　　Morris J teamster bds 112
　　　　Greene
　　William Louis J pressman
　　　　PpubCO bds 112 Greene
MONTE　Johanna C rem to Bridge-
　　　　port CT
　　Louis G art instructor h 28
　　　　Myrtle
MONTEATH　Robert carp h 7 = 65
　　　　Pine
MONTEFUSCO　Giovanni lab h
　　　　395 Water
MONTEGUTI　Augusto lab h 169
　　　　Union
MONTESE　Domenico lab h 15
　　　　Summer
　　Ernest lab h 1 Goyette pl

MONTEVERDE　Della seamstress
　　　　bds 52 Summer
　　Louis rem to Chicago Ill
　　Margherita wid Luigi h 52
　　　　Summer
　　Vistor bds 52 Summer
MONTGOMERY　Charles E. clk
　　　　Boston h 102 Princeton
　　John emp HmfgCo bds 96 Wil-
　　　　braham rd
　　Thomas C sales mgr h 26 East
　　　　Alvord av
MONTMENY　Armond J letter
　　　　carrier bds 18 Colton
　　Eugene emp NEWCo h 18 Noble
MONTOLEONI　Giuseppe lab h 9
　　　　Union
**MONTONARI**　Alberto mach h
　　　　298 Tyler
　　Chaturo emp HmfgCo h 145
　　　　Colton
MONTOVANI　Camille millner bds
　　　　30 Allen

There are two different spellings for the surname Montanari/Montonari in this example, but they are separated by nine other surnames and could easily be overlooked. Keep in mind that the original information was probably handwritten, just like the census, and interpretation of the writing can result in misspellings when the information is alphabetized.

**There are other parts of the directories that are helpful.** In the beginning of the directory, there should be an index to the book listing the contents and the related page numbers. Some of the items listed might be Aldermen, Assessors, Associations, Banks, Cemetery, Churches, Clergymen, Grand Army of the Republic, Justices of the Peace, Medical Examiners, news-

**Important**

papers, Odd Fellows, Orphan Girls' Home, Physicians, Public and Private Schools, Street Directory (an alphabetical listing of the streets within the scope of the directory), Undertakers, Ward Boundaries, and more. Where else will you find a list of all the churches, undertakers, and cemeteries that exist within any geographic area in a specific year? Large urban areas continue to grow year after year, and there may be hundreds of churches now within the boundaries. Knowing which ones existed in 1900 can help narrow the possibilities. The same goes for cemeteries and undertakers. The amount of information is almost endless once you begin to look at the entire directory (see Figure 7-2 on page 94).

The section listed as a "Street Directory" or "Criss Cross Directory" in the index might also have listings of the heads of households at each house on that street. Not all directories have such a listing, but it is always wise to check. The 1917 Springfield, Massachusetts, directory has such a listing, which looks like this:

**COLTON. from 33 Wilbraham rd; south to 28 Beacon, Wards 4 and 5**

**10 Vacant Store**
*38 Monroe st intersects*
39 Conway James J flour feed and grain
41 Brown John H
45 Meyrick Harry K
46 Walker Edson
47 McCleary John & Sons slate roofers
52 Wrightmeyer William L
53 Collier William tailor
54 Alport Lisle I scrap iron
55 Fox Peter P chair caner

59 Schrade John F
59 White George H
71 City of Springfield Water Dept.
*74 Water st intersects*
[some numbers eliminated]
**145 Montonari Chaturo**
146 Stanton Augustus
147 O'Connor Thomas
150 Lucia Pasquale
151 McCarthy Dennis
**154 Artioli Augusto**
155 Sloboda Frank J.

The importance of this list became evident when I noticed the name Augusto Artioli several houses away from Chaturo Montonari. Augusto was Chaturo Montonari's brother-in-law. The two men were married to sisters. Remember, our ancestors did not live in alphabetical order and you need to look at the entire neighborhood to see who might show up. This "picture" of the neighborhood shows many small businesses as well as residences on Colton Street. This street appears to be a typical street for an

**Figure 7-2**
Table of contents from the Springfield, MA, city directory, 1930.

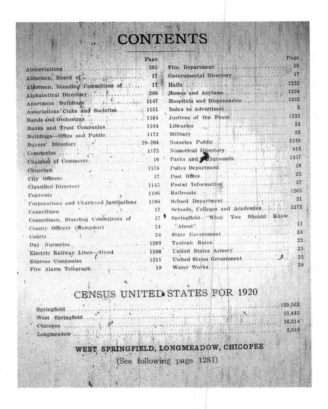

urban area of the period—businesses and houses mixed together. It provides a nice vignette of the area for a specific year.

The additional clues in this example are the cross street names. Many of our ancestors, especially later immigrants living in urban areas, usually lived within a few blocks of each other. Looking at the listed individuals on any of the cross streets might yield more relatives that you might not think to look for in the alphabetical surname section. You might also notice specific ethnicities to certain neighborhoods.

**When the table of contents lists "Clergymen," you might be able to determine which of the churches your ancestor attended.** Look at the marriage record for your ancestor to see if an officiating clergyman is named. You can then look in the directory for that year to see which church he is associated with. Further research in the church records can yield additional family records. One record I found included a copy of a birth record from a village in Italy, thereby identifying the village of origin for the family.

I have encountered many notations for deceased residents as well. When looking in the directories you should not stop when you encounter the first directory without the individual listed. Look at several subsequent years if they are available. After losing my individual in two consecutive directories, the following year's directory listed the following:

**Research Tip**

Fayes Antonio J. deceased Oct. 28, 1878
Fayes Antonio J Mrs. widow, house Washington near Jewett

Had I stopped with the last directory Antonio was listed in, I would have missed this important piece of information. Later years listed his widow by her given name, providing additional information to investigate. Death certificates, cemetery records, and a published obituary rounded out my finds with just this one source.

If your ancestor owned or ran a business, you might look for advertisements in the directories. These can be a fun addition to your family history. The list goes on and on when you start looking at the directory differently. As with the census records, you should look at every possible year available and every section of the directory to be sure you've squeezed every bit of information out of this source before moving on.

## CHURCH RECORDS

If town- or state-recorded vital records were not required or have been lost over the years, you might have to look at church records. What churches existed in the town or county when your ancestor lived there? If city directories are not available for the time period in question, look for town or county histories. Many contain lists of churches, founding dates, and lists of clergy, as well as community members who served as deacons or in some other fashion. You can quickly rule out some of the churches if you know the religion of your ancestor.

Church records, unlike vital records, are always considered private. They are the property of the church and aren't necessarily accessible to you. Again, each church creates and enforces their own rules as it pertains to their records. Some religions maintain archives that house the older records of their parishes, while others will keep the records in the individual churches. You may or may not be allowed access to these records, but it is always worth a try.

Whenever I approach a church in the hopes of finding records relating to my ancestors, I take into consideration that I don't have the right to access them. I'm always grateful when the clergy or staff in any given church assists me in getting records. Be sure you ask for specific information. Most church staff members will not be able to undertake extensive searches through all of their records without some precise information from you. That said, you should always consider a monetary donation to the church. This is especially important if they don't charge you for the search or documents. Most churches are run on limited budgets and donations are always appreciated. You should also never just "drop in" on a church—always make an appointment or make contact in advance. You will have better luck if you take their schedule into consideration.

As with any source, you should know what to expect before using the records. Ask yourself what types of records the specific denomination might have. Catholic churches might have, in addition to christening, marriage, and death records, records for first communion, confirmation, and other rites within the church. You may also discover that a church doesn't have the records for the time period you need but they can direct you to them. I always verify that any facility has the records I need before I visit.

Once you determine the possible religion of your ancestors, you'll need to find out which church they attended. To do this you might have to look to the family information that you acquired early in your research. Do you know which church your parents or grandparents were married in? What church performed the funerals of relatives? The answers to these questions will give you a place to start. Some families attend the same church for generations while other families may attend several different ones during their lifetime. As individuals moved to new locations, the availability of their church of choice was often limited and they may have attended a different denomination of the same church or an entirely different church altogether. Being aware of this is helpful when determining which churches to look at. Keep in mind that rural areas usually had fewer churches than urban areas.

**Tip**

**Church records are especially important if you are dealing with immigrant ancestors.** Catholic churches in urban areas often had an ethnicity attached to them. Immigration from predominantly Catholic countries caused a large increase in the numbers of Catholic parishes, especially in urban areas. In these areas, especially at the turn of the century (1800s–1900s), city directories should, whenever possible, be used to locate the neighborhood church and its ethnic affiliation, if it had one. There may have been a Catholic Church just for Italians, Irish, French, or Portuguese. While all may be Roman Catholic, each of these ethnic groups had their own beliefs and customs that they wished to continue in their newly adopted country.

When an ethnicity is attached to a church, the records can be even more valuable. If an Italian-born individual got married in such a church, there may be records from the church or town in the old country included with the local records. I've found copies of birth and baptismal certificates included with marriage and death records. This is especially important if you do not know the village or parish of origin for your immigrant ancestors. You'll also find that the names of the individuals and the towns they came from are more often spelled correctly. Many of our immigrant ancestors were illiterate but the ethnic priest would likely know the correct spelling of the names and locations. The church records may also contain the names of the sponsors of a child, witnesses to the marriage, etc., which don't appear on the vital records and may offer clues to other relatives or close family friends.

There are also different types of Catholic churches. The most common of these is the Roman Catholic Church, but there are also Ruthenian and Orthodox Catholic churches to consider. In addition to Catholic churches, you will also have various denominations of Protestant, Mormon, Episcopalian, and other religions. It always amazes me how many different religions exist in our society. Each of these churches will have different records, depending on the rites and sacraments they perform.

If your ancestors lived in urban areas, as many immigrants did, you will need to determine what churches of their faith were in the area during their lifetime. To do this check a city directory for the time period to see what churches are listed. If you have a marriage or other certificate signed by a clergyman, the city directory can also be used to determine his church affiliation. By looking at the directory and checking a street map, you may be able to narrow down which church your ancestors were most likely attending. Keep in mind that most urban residents didn't drive or even own a car, so walking distance or public transportation was an important factor when choosing a church.

Once you have determined which churches existed in the place and time period of interest, see if they are still in operation today. If not, you'll need to find out where the records are housed. In some cases, churches or parishes may have merged and the records may be kept in the new combined church. They may also be deposited in a church archive, perhaps local, state, or national in scope. You will have to do some investigating to locate the records if you hope to access them.

Many records have been lost to fire, water, and other disasters over the centuries, so many may not exist at all. Some records have been microfilmed (early Quaker records) and are accessible though some libraries and the Family History Library in Salt Lake City and their Family History Centers around the world. **Quaker records are some of the most fascinating.** Marriages oftentimes list all of the people attending the wedding. When a Quaker moves from one geographic area to another, there may be letters of removal

**Internet Source**

For help locating church records, check Cyndi's List <www.cyndislist.com> under "church records" or US-GenWeb <www.usgenweb.org> for the state and locality of interest.

**Sources**

and acceptance to the new church. There are also Women's and Men's meeting records, which may include reprimands for unacceptable behavior.

Many denominations of churches do maintain archives of older records. These archives may be located in the same state as the local church or may be more national in scope. If the church you are interested in no longer has some of the older records (they only have so much storage space), ask where the records were sent. Regardless of which religious denomination you are researching, always check the Family History Library (FHL) catalog to see if any records have been microfilmed. The FHL has wonderful histories of different churches, lists of clergymen, registers of members, and other such records among their collection. When you access the FHL catalog online <www.familysearch.org>, search for records under the denomination and the state of interest. (See *Your Guide to the Family History Library* by Paula Stuart Warren and James W. Warren.)

## CEMETERY RECORDS

As with church records, cemetery records may or may not be considered public records. Many cemeteries are the property of, or are maintained by, a specific church, while others may be town- or city-owned and operated. This makes a big difference in the availability of records. Due to the large number of people researching their ancestry, some churches and cemeteries have been inundated with requests for information. As a result, some now charge for information, and many only provide information in response to written requests. This is understandable when you consider how many requests they receive, how small the staff is, and how many duties they must attend to daily in regards to current cemetery business.

When you do request information, you should be looking for the names of all the individuals buried in a plot, be it a family plot or a multigrave plot. The people buried there might provide clues to the maiden name of the wife or the names of other relatives. If they are buried together, there is probably some connection. There may also be individuals buried in the plot whose names do not appear on the gravestone. Not everyone could afford a stone or to have engraving done. You will encounter many unmarked gravesites. The only way you will know if an ancestor is buried there is through the cemetery records.

Once you have located the cemetery (this information appears on some death certificates) and found out where the grave is located, you should copy all of the information from the stone as well as take photos of it from

**For More Info**

**CHURCH AND CEMETERY RESEARCH**

For more on the records, see *Your Guide to Cemetery Research*, by Sharon DeBartolo Carmack (Cincinnati: Betterway Books, 2002) and *U.S. Catholic Sources: A Diocesan Research Guide*, by Virginia Humling (Salt Lake City: Ancestry, Inc., 1995).

several angles. Pay close attention to the names on the gravestones in the vicinity of the one you're interested in. Take pictures of them and note any symbols carved on the stone, as these may indicate occupation, membership in fraternal organizations, or military service. Many extended families bought plots together, and relatives might be buried nearby. This is especially true of older cemeteries in rural areas. I have found many unknown relatives simply by reading nearby stones. When taking pictures in the cemetery, make sure to include one showing the topography of the land around the stone. This can assist future generations if they go looking for the grave later. You might even find, as I have, that you need these reminders when you go back several years later. By including roadways, large monuments, or nearby buildings in the photo, you will have a better idea of the placement of the grave in relationship to the area.

Tip

One final reminder about church and cemetery research. **If you are assisted by a helpful clerk who provides you with information without charging you for it, leave a donation of some sort (never less than $5).** The information is important to you, so why not make a donation as a way of thanking the clerk? This small act of appreciation will go a long way. If you need to go back to that cemetery or church (and you will most likely have to at some point), hopefully you will be remembered for being appreciative of their efforts on your behalf. Remember that you only get one chance to make a first impression.

## UNDERTAKER'S RECORDS

Other records that go hand-in-hand with those of the church and cemetery are undertaker's records, depending on the time period in which the death took place. Look on the death certificate, in the obituary, or in the death notice for mention of an undertaker or funeral home. Search the city directories for those years to see how many funeral homes were actually in the area. Check records for other family members to see if a specific funeral home was used by more than one relative. Many families continue to use the same funeral home for several generations.

Once you have the name of the undertaker, you should determine if he is still in business. There are several specialized directories available in many libraries listing funeral directors. Most of these directories are national in scope. Two such books are *The National Yellow Book* and *American Blue Book of Funeral Directors*. There are others that are similar but vary in layout or title. Another place to locate funeral homes and undertakers that were in business over the last century or more is in city directories.

Funeral directors can also be very helpful in learning about regional funerary customs and locations of cemeteries in rural areas. One funeral home in Vermont was extremely helpful when I was unable to locate a burial plot within the cemetery listed on a death certificate. After driving and walking through the rather large cemetery and not locating a stone, I realized, as I was driving out of the cemetery, that the funeral home listed on the death certificate was just across the street. I stopped and rang the bell, hoping to find someone there. A young man answered the door and invited me in. When I explained my dilemma he asked to look at the death certificate I had. Upon closer examination he said he couldn't offer any further information, but that his grandfather might have handled the services in that year and called him at home. After his grandfather asked a few questions about the certificate, the young man hung up. Handing the certificate back to me he said, "The certificate states that the deceased was entombed in the neighboring cemetery, not interred." I was really confused! He then explained that burials didn't occur in Vermont during the winter months because of the frozen ground. The deceased had been placed in the cemetery's tomb (the only one within a fifty-mile radius) until spring. Once burial could take place the deceased was moved to his hometown, twenty-eight miles away, for final burial. I drove to the hometown cemetery and immediately found his gravestone. The knowledge of the undertaker provided me with the information I needed. Another mystery solved!

**EIGHT**

# What's Next?

## LAND AND PROBATE RECORDS

I n some cases, land and probate records are maintained in the same location (courthouse, town hall, etc.). Different states keep them in different places, so you'll have to do some research to find out where they are. In many cases these records, or at least the earlier ones, have been recorded in copybooks and many have been microfilmed.

**Copybooks are large volumes that the original records are transcribed into.** Most microfilms of probate records are of these copybooks, since they're easier to film, and not of the originals. Microfilms of land records will always be of the copybooks. The reason for this is when a land transfer is concluded, the actual deed remains with the person who has purchased the land. It is then, hopefully, recorded in the copybook at the courthouse or town hall that has jurisdiction over that piece of land.

If a deceased individual owned property, it is especially important to look for a record of the estate settlement. You will need to determine which court or authority in your specific state of interest handles such affairs. In New England they are referred to as probate courts, in New York as surrogate courts, in Mississippi as orphans courts, and in Iowa the records are held in the county clerk's office.

\di'fin\ *vb*

**Definitions**

### Land Records

Our ancestors often owned very few material goods during their lifetime, and land was probably the most valuable asset any individual might possess. Because of this, land records are very detailed. Most researchers are

**For More Info**

**BOOKS FOR LAND AND PROBATE RESEARCH**

*Locating Your Roots: Discover Your Ancestors Using Land Records*, by Patricia Law Hatcher (Cincinnati: Betterway Books, 2003)

*Wills and Other Probate Records: A Practical guide to Researching Your Ancestors' Last Documents* (Keeper of the Public Record, 2004)

*The Genealogist's Question & Answer Book*, by Marcia D. Melnyk (Cincinnati: Betterway Books, 2002)

amazed at the legal language contained in these documents, no matter how early the time period. If one of your ancestors owned property, whether it was a house or a farm, there will be documents recording the acquisition and disposal of the property at the governmental division with authority over the property's location. These records, like so many others, are recorded and maintained at different locations in different states. Some states maintain the land records at the town level, others at the county level, and there are some land records that are maintained at the state or federal level. Like every other record that you have learned about, the rules and regulations vary by state, territory, and original owner of the specific land.

You may find clues to land ownership in any number of records, but the United States federal census records from 1850 through 1930 (except for 1880 and 1890), which indicated if a person owned property, can be some of the most valuable. Because the census lists the town, county, and state that the individual resides in, you will have a place to start. Check to see where the land records are held in that state and take it from there.

## LAND/PROPERTY TERMINOLOGY

- *bounty land*—land that was granted in lieu of monetary payment for military service

- *deed*—the document that legally transfers ownership of property from one individual (the grantor) to another (grantee). The original deed remains in the hands of the buyer.

- *grantee*—the purchaser of the property

- *grantor*—the seller of the property

- *quit-claim*—a document by which an individual releases his claim to property and transfers it to another

- *registered deed*—one that has been recorded in the official record book with jurisdiction over the property transferred

Land records from the initial settlement of the state or colony might appear in proprietors' records. When a group of individuals obtained a charter or patent for land to establish a town, the land would be given to the group, whose members were called proprietors. The state or government that claimed ownership of the land would issue the charter or patent, and the land would then be divided among qualified individuals based on family size, or possibly wealth, for homes and farms. Some jurisdictions would have a specific requirement that a home, farm, or improvements be completed within a certain timeframe. Land was also set aside for a meeting house or church, with other land left in the hands of the proprietors for public use. This initial distribution of land will usually appear in the town records rather than the land records.

When the federal government was established after the Revolutionary War, the lands not already distributed (mostly in the Midwest, South, and Southwest) became known as public domain lands, owned by the United States Government. This land was used as payment for military service (bounty land) or sold to individuals wishing to settle it. Some of this land was granted to individuals under the Homestead Act of 1862. This act provided settlers with 160 acres of land if they cultivated it and improved it over a period of five years. The settler was then exempt from any cash payments for the land. He did, however, have to meet certain age and citizenship criteria. Many settlers in the Midwest acquired their property in this way.

Once an individual had legal possession of a piece of land, he had the right to sell it. This process created land deeds and records necessary for authorities to identify the legal owner of the land and to levy taxes on the property. Land transfer records involve two parties—the grantor (seller) and the grantee (buyer). It is important to check all available indexes and every land transfer when researching an individual. Keep in mind that there are two types of indexes available in most cases. One is called the "Grantee from Grantor" and the other is the "Grantor to Grantee." Sometimes they are referred to as "Direct (seller) or Indirect (buyer)" indexes. Since there are two parties participating in any land transaction, you need to look for your subject as both a seller (grantee/indirect) or as a buyer (grantor/direct). Make sure that you look at every record available for that individual.

**Land records, as I mentioned before, are available to researchers in the copybooks and on microfilm (of the copybooks) only.** Often you can use the indexes first, determine which records you need to review, and then either order the microfilmed records (if available) or contact the office or court holding the records to obtain a copy. From the index you will know the volume and page number and perhaps the date, making it far easier for the clerk to locate the record for you.

Some land records will be basic and may not provide additional data,

**Microfilm Source**

**For More Info**

**BOOKS ON LAND RECORDS**

*Land & Property Research in the United States,* by E. Wade Home (Salt Lake City: Ancestry, Inc., 1997)

*Locating Your Roots: Discover your ancestors using land records,* by Patricia Law Hatcher (Cincinnati: Betterway Books, 2003)

but there are others that list the provenance or history of the land. I have found deeds that state how, when, and from whom the land was acquired, listing owners back to the original proprietor. This can be valuable information if the land was acquired in settlement of an estate (see the Joseph A. Rogers example below). If the person buying or selling is not a resident of that locality, their place of legal residence may be listed. Deeds will also contain a description of the specific parcel of land or refer you back to a previous deed for the description. The description may also contain the names of the abutting property owners. This can be valuable information, especially in the precensus years. As with any record, you never know what might appear in any single transaction.

In one case, I was trying to determine the parentage of my ancestor, Joseph A. Rogers. His gravestone states he was born in 1813 and died in 1853. I couldn't find a birth or death record for him, and only had his marriage record from 1839 and his listing in the 1850 Vermont census. The 1850 census lists Joseph's birthplace as New Hampshire. I decided to look at all of the known Joseph Rogers living in New England (concentrating on New Hampshire and Vermont first) that were born about 1810 and were deceased by 1853. I began with a list of thirty-eight individuals. I slowly worked my way through the list, eliminating them one by one. During this process I came across a Rogers/Rodgers family living in Thetford, Orange County, Vermont, that piqued my interest. Thetford is right on the Connecticut River and only the river separates it from New Hampshire. While I could not find a man named Joseph in the proper time period, I did find a man named Constant Rogers, who married in 1811 in Thetford. This individual caught my eye since my great-grandfather, Joseph's son, was named Hoxey Constant Rogers in 1842. Joseph's wife, Annie Delilah Barber, was the daughter of Hoxey Rogers and Nancy Emery. If they used one grandfather's name why not both?

I next looked for a probate record for Constant Rogers and his wife Love Sanborn (Cummings) Rogers, to no avail. After their marriage in Thetford, they disappear and were not buried along with the other family members in the local cemeteries. Without a probate, how could I determine what children Constant and Love Rogers had? Perhaps the land records might help.

When I looked through the indexes for Thetford land transfers (Vermont keeps land records at the town level), I tracked Constant Rogers' activity. The last time he was recorded in the Thetford records was in 1823. I made a list of all transfers to and from Constant Rogers. I then checked the same indexes for Joseph Rogers' name. One record jumped out at me. A Joseph A. Rogers was selling land to a man named Noah Ellis. There was a transfer from Constant Rogers to a Noah Ellis as well. Could Noah Ellis be a link? When I obtained a copy of an 1833 transfer, I realized I had hit the jackpot!

My Joseph Rogers always signed deeds, records, etc. as Joseph A. Rogers. I don't know what the "A" stands for, but thankfully he always used it. The land record states in part: "I Joseph A. Rodgers of Thetford in Orange County and state of Vermont for the consideration of sixty dollars paid to my full satisfaction by Noah Ellis of Thetford in Orange County and State of Vermont . . . a certain piece of land in Thetford aforesaid as described as follows viz: all the right title or interest that shall or may fall to me as heir to the estate of Constant Rodgers formerly of said Thetford deceased meaning to convey all of the interest that may fall to me as heir to the estate of Widow Mehitable Rodgers what was set off to her as her right of dower of the estate of Samuel Rodgers late of said Thetford, deceased . . . I am the sole owner of the premises and have good right and title to convey the same."

Further investigation showed that the land Joseph was selling to Noah Ellis actually bounded the land sold to Noah in 1823 by Constant Rogers. This was the last record I found for Joseph A. Rogers in Thetford, and he appeared in Mount Holly, Rutland County, Vermont, when he married in 1839. This, in addition to another member of the extended Rogers family from Thetford appearing in Mount Holly around the same time period, helped to solve the mystery of Joseph's parentage, although I have still not been able to locate a birth or death record for him. The two land records also helped me to determine that Constant Rogers died sometime between 1823 and 1833. Because Joseph stated that he was heir to the estate and the sole owner of the land, it leads me to believe that he was the only surviving child of Constant and Love Rogers/Rodgers. The name Rogers/ Rodgers appears simultaneously in the records, and I am confident that they are referring to the same family. Subsequent records, including a Revolutionary War pension record for Joseph's grandmother, Mehitable Rogers (the widow of Samuel Rogers), in 1837 spell the name "Rogers." In 1837 Mehitable was living, along with several of Constant's siblings, in the Eastern Townships in Canada.

This case study should reinforce the idea that every possible record must be looked at. Don't overlook land or probate records for any and all family

**\di'fin\ vb**

Definitions

**RIGHT OF DOWER**

Dower: that portion of an estate which is given to a widow by law from her deceased husband's estate to be used for her lifetime (*A to ZAX: A Comprehensive Dictionary for Genealogists & Historians, Third Edition,* by Barbara Jean Evans Hearthside Press, 1995).

members because you never know what you'll find. Always do a complete transcription of the written record to be sure you haven't missed anything!

## Probate Records

Probate records can be some of your most revealing sources. Nothing will give you a better picture of an individual's life like an estate inventory. This inventory is taken after a person dies and his estate is being settled. The person's assets will be listed, along with the value of the possessions and any debts owed by the individual. Not all people will have an estate to settle but it is always worth a look. You may be lucky enough to find a will listing the relatives and bequests given to particular people, or you might find one that is brief at best and lists no names at all.

Probate or estate records are the records created after a person's death to determine the value and distribution of all assets of the deceased. You will need to check the locality of interest to determine where these records are recorded and what else they might be called. In some New England states the official jurisdiction is in the county courthouse, while in others it is in a designated probate district or at the town level. In other states, such as New York, these records are handled in the Surrogate's Court (after 1787) and before that by the State Court.

Always look to see if any of these records or indexes have been microfilmed. Utilizing microfilmed indexes to determine if the record you seek actually exists is a fairly easy task. **You can order and use the films at any one of the thousands of Family History Centers around the world.** Once you have selected the records you wish to see from the index, you can then move on to the records themselves. If films or the copybooks are available, use them first to determine that it is indeed the record you are looking for. You can order the microfilm that contains the actual records (if they have been filmed). When you look at that film you'll be able to see if it's a copy of the original probate package (also called a probate docket) or just the copybooks. If the microfilm of the probate records shows many separate pieces of paper, then you are most likely looking at the original probate packet. Many pieces of paper make up the file, since probate packets are accumulated over the time period it takes to settle the estate. At times, settlement can take many years.

I will always look at microfilmed copybooks first and rule a record in or out before I will use the original probate packet. There are several reasons for this. First of all, the microfilms are likely available at your local

**Money Saver**

Family History Center or state library. I can, in most cases, determine if the record actually pertains to my research subject from the information contained in the copybook. Once I know that it does—and only then— will I go to the courthouse or repository and look at the originals. I have discovered over the years that not all of the little slips of paper contained in the packet are transcribed into the copybooks. Many of these papers are brittle with age and should be handled carefully and only when neces- sary. Using the originals *only* after determining that they are pertinent will help to preserve these records for future researchers. Every researcher must use the utmost care when handling such originals. Use only one file at a time, carefully unfold and refold any papers you use, and use discretion when it comes to photocopying any such records. If the paper cannot be safely flattened, do not expose it to the photocopier. If in doubt, consult the clerk or a staff member of the facility.

When reviewing documents from a probate or estate settlement file, pay special attention to the estate inventory. If you read it carefully you can actually visualize how the person taking the inventory walked from room to room, listing the entire contents of the household. It's very interesting to see just how much, or how little, our ancestors possessed in previous eras. What they possessed can be interesting as well. Barrels of whiskey, hard cider, and the like are not uncommon. Kitchen goods usually consisted of a few pans and plates, a few pieces of silverware, a tea kettle, and perhaps a few towels. Beds might be accompanied with one set of linens, or two if the individual was more prosperous. Clothing usually consisted of only a couple pairs of pants, perhaps one jacket, and a pair of boots. When you read the sparse contents of such a modest homestead, certain items like mirrors (looking glasses), Bibles, and china really give you a feeling for the priorities and perhaps the economic status of your ancestor. Fascinating stuff!

When looking at probate records, you might locate a will written or signed by the deceased. A will can be a simple document, with no specific individuals named, or very explicit in nature. Some wills are so exacting in their requirements that I have often wondered if the deceased trusted his heirs to carry out his wishes. **If a person died intestate (without a will), there may still be estate or probate records.** The estate may be insolvent (insufficient value to pay off debts) or may contain property and personal estate that must be inventoried and distributed. Sometimes estate settle- ments when a will has not been left can be far more informative than those containing wills. Be ready for surprises, no matter what records you use.

**Research Tip**

## PROBATE/ESTATE TERMINOLOGY

- *administrator*—a person appointed by the court to dispose of the estate when the individual dies intestate (without a will) or fails to name an executor or a person appointed to manage the estate of an incompetent person

- *dower*—the portion of the estate that is reserved by law (when the deceased dies intestate) for the support of the wife (and children) during her lifetime

- *dower right*—the portion of the estate that is given to the widow for her use during her lifetime

- *executor/executrix*—the man/woman named by the deceased to dispose of the estate

- *intestate*—when a person dies without leaving a valid will

- *insolvent*—when an estate has insufficient money or assets to pay the debts owed

- *inventory*—a listing of a deceased's assets including real estate and their value

- *testate*—when a person dies leaving a valid will

- *testator*—the person making the will

- *will and testament*—a will is the document with which the testator distributes his real estate and the testament is the document which distributes his personal estate

For example, the will of my great-great-grandmother, Rebecca Emery (See Figure 8-1 on page 109) is particularly unusual for several reasons. It shows interesting aspects not often found in the time period (1863). First of all, it's one of the few wills I've found for a female ancestor, and it contains a prenuptial agreement, a codicil, and confirmation that my great-grandmother, Teresa, was an adopted daughter of the deceased. The original will states ". . . I give & devise to Hoxxey Barber of said Walpole all the real estate which may belong to me at the time of my decease—To have & to hold the same to him during the term of his natural life; provided the marriage contemplated between said Barber & my self shall be solemnized . . ."

Rebecca states that she wishes to leaves to "Teresa Rebecca Emery, who now lives with me as an adopted daughter, all of the real estate aforesaid" and "all my books & wearing apparel." It wasn't common for women

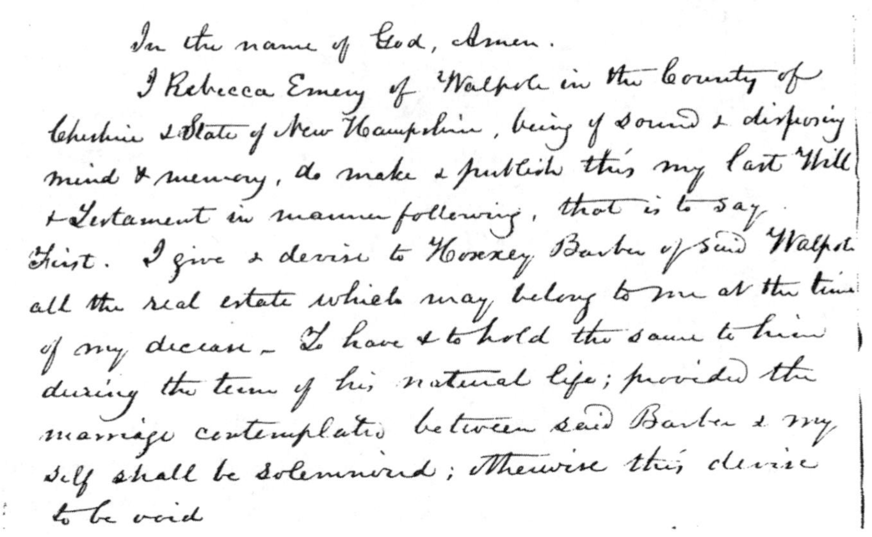

**Figure 8-1**
Rebecca Emery's will and transcription.

WILL OF REBECCA (BROWN) (STEARNS) (EMERY) BARBER—
CHESHIRE CO., NH PROBATE

In the name of God, Amen.

I Rebecca Emery of Walpole in the County of / Cheshire & State of New Hampshire, / being of sound & disposing / mind & memory, do make and publish this my last Will / & Testament in manner following, that is to say. / First. I give & devise to Hoxxey Barber of said Walpole / all the real estate which may belong to me at the time / of my decease - To have & to hold the same to him / during the term of his natural life; provided the / marriage contemplated between said Barber & my / self shall be solemnized; otherwise this devise / to be void /

of that era to be educated, let alone own books. Obviously my great-grandmother's love of reading was engrained in her throughout her life by her mother.

Rebecca also makes bequests to her brothers, Thomas and Obadiah Brown, her sisters Harriet Brown and Mary Hall, and her nephew, James E. Marshall, indicating she had another sister who married a Marshall. Rebecca then adds a codicil to the original will sixteen months later, revoking all legacies to her siblings and nephew and giving their shares to her new husband, Hoxxey [sic] Barber.

As stated previously, some estates can take decades to settle. I actually found a probate record in Rutland County, Vermont, for a Stephen Nichols that began in 1788 and was not completed until 1841—fifty-three years later! (See the case study below.) It is important to check the indexes carefully to see if there are later records that also pertain to the same estate.

**Case Study**

## CASE STUDY

In the case of Stephen Nichols, his will was written on 25 September 1787 and presented to the Rutland County, Vermont, court on 18 March 1788. The original will provided almost no valuable information other than placing his death between the two dates. He named his wife, Anna, and left his entire estate to her during her lifetime, after which it was to be "equally shared among my children." He does not list how many, the sex, or the names of his children. One important thing to notice is that he calls them "my children" and does not state that they are Anna's children as well. Be aware of the wording. What is not said can be as helpful as what is.

Stephen also appointed his "good friends Rowland Stafford and John Stafford, both of Danby" to be "executors in trust for my children," indicating that the children are probably still minors. Further research showed that Rowland and John were the brothers of Stephen Nichols' wife, Nancy "Anna" Stafford.

The subsequent inventory of the estate provided some great clues. Not only did the inventory include a Bible, indicating Stephen was a religious man, but it also included a set of shoemaker's tools. This might indicate an occupation above and beyond the occupation of farming he mentions in his will. It is important to pay close attention to every detail of the inventory. In addition to his worldly goods, the inventory lists many debts, both owed to his estate as well as owed by it.

The list of debts included names of individuals that should be looked at thoroughly. They include a Joseph Nickels, Philip Nickels, Beloved Carpenter, Palmer Stafford and several others. Since Stephen Nichols' parentage is not known, the Nickels individuals are of particular interest. Keep in mind that there was really no standard spelling of names in that era and Nickels and Nichols are probably the same name.

My ultimate goal was to determine if this Stephen Nichols was the father of my ancestor, Drusilla Nichols. Drusilla and her sister, Katie, married brothers Joseph and William Carpenter. The fact that Beloved Carpenter, a relative of Joseph and William, shows up in the inventory is encouraging and worth further research. All of these clues came out of the original will and probate record from 1788.

While looking at the index to probates in Rutland County, Vermont, I noticed another Stephen Nichols probate listed in 1840. At first I did not consider this record. Later I thought that perhaps Stephen Nichols had a son named after him, so I looked at the 1840 record. Imagine my surprise when I realized that it was a continuation of the 1788 probate.

According to the 1840 record, Stephen and Nancy "Anna" Nichols had five daughters named Elcy, Drusilla, Catherine, Patty, and Barbara. The record also identified Drusilla as the wife of Joseph Carpenter and Catherine as the wife of William Carpenter, thereby confirming the parentage of Drusilla and Catherine. Since all but one of the daughters were married by 1840, the papers provided their husbands' names as well. Only Barbara was unmarried and she was the one that initiated the 1840 probate record.

"The undersigned Barbary Nichols of Danby one of the heirs of the estate of Stephen Nichols formerly of Harwich, since named Mount Tabor, deceased respectfully represents that she is entitled to one undivided fifth part of said estate and being desirous to hold the same in severalty she prays the Court to order a division of the said estate and to appoint a committee for that purpose."

The document was dated March 1840 and witnessed by Isaac Nichols—another Nichols individual to look at. What caused Barbara Nichols to petition the court at such a late date? Why had she not gotten or taken her share as stated in the original will and probate? Additional research provided the answers. After Stephen Nichols' death in 1787 or 1788, his widow remarried a man by the name of Joseph Bull in 1790. Joseph was a widower with five children ranging in age from fourteen to three years of age when he married Nancy (Stafford) Nichols. Joseph Bull and Nancy then had five children together (and possibly others). Nancy died on 10 Jan 1840. In all probability, Barbara lived with her mother all of the years after her father's death and never had a need to legally obtain her share of the estate. Upon the death of her mother in 1840, she might have had concerns that the estate would go to not only Nancy's children by her first marriage but also to Joseph's children by his previous marriage and to their children together. She petitioned the court to receive her fair share of her father's estate, thereby generating all of the paperwork that solved the parentage question so well.

Once I had determined that the record was pertinent to my research, I went to the courthouse that held the original record to review the entire probate packet. There were several additional papers that were not recorded in the copybook. One paper was a note from the court that said

*"April 24th 1788 gave directions to John Stafford and Rowland Stafford to notify the creditor to Stephen Nichols estate to exhibit their claims by the 18th March 1789 to post up an advertisement in Danby and Stephentown State of New York and in the Bennington Papers 3 weeks."*

This small piece of paper provided three additional locations to research. The court, by requiring the notice to be posted in all three places, indicates that Stephen Nichols either lived or did business in those localities. Any creditors from those locations wouldn't have seen a notice posted only in Danby, Vermont. The purpose of the notice is to give anyone with a claim against the estate notice and time to respond. Always watch for such notices or mention of other locations.

Probate records must be thoroughly dissected and every piece of information must be used to further the research. Do not overlook anything! Just as in the census records, you must look at every single particle of information and read between the lines.

## NEWSPAPERS

Newspapers are a wonderful resource for family historians. Looking at a single edition of the local newspaper provides you with a snapshot of one day in that time and place. I have always enjoyed reading newspapers from previous decades. You will see advertising that will make you chuckle; information regarding food and home prices; reports of local, national, and world events; social and church events; death notices; announcements for births and marriages; and a myriad of other useful items.

Under the United States Newspaper Program, one library in each state is designated as the repository for copies (paper or microfilm copies) of all extant (surviving) newspapers for that state. Many such facilities hold newspaper collections from other states as well, but you want to know what they have for your state or locality of interest. In some cases the repository will be the state library or one of the larger public libraries. To determine which facility holds this collection in any given state, the District of Columbia, Puerto Rico, or the U.S. Virgin Islands, go to the United States Newspaper Program Web site <www.neh.gov/projects/usnp.html>. This site also explains the program in depth. Many of the libraries that hold microfilm copies participate in the interlibrary loan program as well.

**Many researchers will use newspapers when looking for death notices or obituaries, but they often overlook other possibilities.** Check the local paper around the time of significant family events such as graduations, twenty-

Warning

fifth or fiftieth wedding anniversaries, baptisms, engagements, marriages, etc. If the local paper is from a small town, you should always be on the lookout for social columns. Newspapers rely on circulation numbers when setting the advertising rates. The best way to get the circulation numbers up is to mention as many residents' names as possible in the paper. Every time a family member is mentioned, whether it is in a school list, engagement announcement, social event, etc., the family buys extra copies to share with other family members living elsewhere. Small town papers are famous for their social columns. Some even detail what people were wearing at a certain event and list the names of all in attendance. This is great stuff for the family historian.

If you know that your ancestor was active in a fraternal organization (Elks, Masonic Lodge, Odd Fellows, etc.), you will want to look for articles involving the local chapters of these groups. The same goes for church socials, fundraising organizations, and school events. If your ancestor owned a business, you might find an interesting advertisement to add color to the family history. Of course you can always look for your ancestors' names in the police notices, court reports, and delinquent tax lists—you never know! The possibilities are almost endless once you get started.

Whenever I am looking for a record in a newspaper, I always take the time to browse the paper for interesting articles or editorials that shed light on the time period, political climate, social customs, and economic status of the day. Remember that a newspaper is a brief glimpse of one or more days in our history and in the life of our ancestors. Consider printing or photocopying an interesting ad showing prices in the grocery store, ads for apartment rentals, clothing ads, etc. These little items will make your family history more interesting and thought provoking.

Of course death notices and obituaries are one of the most used articles in the newspapers of the twentieth century. Most papers, unless they are small town editions, will not have such notices at the turn of the century or earlier. This is especially true for the deaths of women, children, and immigrants. It was common for urban newspapers to record these events for those in the public eye, politicians, business owners, and other well-known individuals. Unfortunately most of our ancestors do not fit into that group. The exception to this rule is in the event of a tragic death or an accident. I have found incredible information for those ancestors who died under strange or tragic circumstances.

The example in chapter five (regarding Saturno Montanari's death) illustrates this. Having been one of two people killed when a freak summer storm hit the city of Springfield, Massachusetts, his death was reported on page one of the paper as a news item, along with a photograph, but there was no death notice, funeral notice, or obituary published. I almost missed the article as I was looking for the death notices and obituaries during the week of his death. I did not see the article until I was rewinding the film! Thankfully the photograph that accompanied the article was a copy of one we have hanging on the wall in our home and it caught my eye. To this day, I now scan every page of a newspaper when I am researching so I will miss nothing of interest.

When you do find a death notice or obituary, you have hit a wonderful resource. These records hold many clues and facts that should lead you to other important records. When you read an obituary or death notice, watch for the following information:

- Names and residences of relatives
- Places of birth or residence
- Name of the church where any services were held
- Name of the cemetery or burial place
- Name of the undertaker or funeral home providing services
- Organizations that the deceased belonged to
- Educational institutions
- Occupations or employers

When you are looking at newspapers, be sure to look at all of the issues (morning and evening editions) for the week following the date of death and funeral. Many times I have found articles detailing the funeral that include thank-you notices from family members for flowers and condolences. I have even found mention of when some relatives left to return home. If burial took place in a different location than the death, the newspaper may mention it after the fact, especially if the body had to be shipped to a distant location.

## CONFERENCES AND NETWORKING

Now that we have discussed some, but certainly not all, of the records you will use in your research, you have a place to start. As you become a more seasoned researcher, you will find additional records and resources to further your goals. **It is important to stay current in your knowledge of the genealogical field of study.** Books, like those which I have mentioned earlier,

Important

are one of your best sources for knowledge. However, records and sources are only as good as the researcher using them. The more you know about the record, its creation, reason for existing, and how to use it, the more successful you will be.

There are many opportunities to further your education and make yourself a better researcher. Many libraries and genealogical societies offer lectures, courses, or workshops. There are local, regional, and national genealogical conferences held year round in the United States. Attending one or more of these conferences can go a long way toward that education. Not only are there lectures and presentations covering a wide variety of subjects, but most conferences also host vendors that cater to the genealogist. Booksellers, software creators and manufacturers, photo restoration experts, Internet companies, and others all sell goods or information to the attendees. You can often try a computer program, find new books, and learn about the newest resources and cutting edge technology at a conference. Where else will you find so many books or goods relating to the subject matter in one place?

One of the most important aspects of both conferences and the Internet is the possibility to network with other researchers. Talking to others who share the same research interests, have encountered the same problems, and used the same records is exciting. For some reason our spouses, children, and other relatives are not always as excited about our research as we are. Another genealogist will always understand how thrilling it is to find great-grandpa's name in that record, book, or cemetery. I find it reassuring that I am not the only person who thinks genealogy and history are exciting.

Determining what conferences or events might be occurring in any given area isn't as difficult as you might think. I hate to keep using the word *Internet*, but when it comes to family history it is hard not to. Large organizations like the New England Historic Genealogical Society (NEHGS), the National Genealogical Society (NGS), and The Federation of Genealogical Societies (FGS) hold conferences annually or biannually all over the country. You can access these societies' home pages to see where and when upcoming conferences will be held. Keeping abreast of what is happening in your own state or area through membership in a local society can also help. Check bulletin boards in libraries with genealogical or historical research rooms for brochures. State archives and the National Archives facilities also display conference brochures. Genealogical magazines and publications often list conference information.

**Notes**

**SOCIETIES AND GROUPS ORGANIZING CONFERENCES**

- Federation of Genealogical Societies <www.fgs .org>

- National Genealogical Society <www.ngsgenealo gy.org>

- The New England Historic Genealogical Society <www.newenglandancestors .org>

- The New England Regional Genealogical Conference <www.rootsweb .com/~manergc>

- Utah Genealogical Association Conference <www .infouga.org/conference .html>

**Printed Source**

### GENEALOGICAL MAGAZINES

- *Ancestry Magazine* <http://shops.ancestry.com/product>

- *Family Chronicle Magazine* <www.familychronicle.com>

- *Family Tree Magazine* <www.familytreemagazine.com>

- *Heritage Quest Magazine* <www.heritagequestmagazine.com>

- *History Magazine* <www.history-magazine.com>

- *National Genealogical Society News Magazine* <www.ngsgenealogy.org/pubsnewsmag.htm>

- *Prologue* (A National Archives and Records Administration publication) <www.archives.gov/publications/prologue/index.html>

Magazines and publications can be your best investment for keeping up with current news in the genealogical field. Because they are published more often than books, they contain more up-to-date information. This is especially true with respect to information regarding Web sites and electronic resources.

## VOLUNTEER OPPORTUNITIES

Another way to keep up on what's happening is to volunteer at one of the research facilities near you. Even if you don't know much about genealogy or the facility's resources, you will learn a great deal by assisting others. I have volunteered at our regional National Archives facility for the last five years or so. I have also volunteered at a local FHC. I probably learned more as a volunteer than by doing my own research. Helping people access records that I haven't had the opportunity to use opened new avenues of research. It's also a wonderful feeling to be a part of a researcher's big find! Just working with the employees and other volunteers will teach you so much about the records and how to use them. Hands-on is the best way to learn.

The family historian will always be learning about new records, methods for research, and technological advances. That is what makes this hobby (or should I say obsession) so interesting. We are constantly learning, sharing, and discovering new ideas and resources. With the many records out there, it can be difficult to remember them all. Using the list provided (see sidebar on page 117), run a check on every person in your ancestry. Have you truly exhausted the available records? Have you missed any? If you've discovered some new resources, add them to the list and share that new resource with others. But most of all, remember to be open to new ideas, new records, and possible chances to learn from others—including your ancestors!

## ADDITIONAL RECORDS

If your ancestors lived in the same geographic area or state as you do, you will be able to access many local records. Most researchers, however, do not enjoy such a luxury. I am grateful that my mother's ancestors landed in New England and stayed here, as it makes my research much easier and more localized. My father's family is another story. They left Italy, settled in New York and New Jersey for a while, and finally settled in Massachusetts. This makes the research a bit more difficult. Just take it one step at a time and always work from the present backward. You will have to learn about what records exist and how to access them in

## CHECKLIST FOR NONHOME RESOURCES

- Archives—State and National
- Cemetery and Undertaker's Records
- Census Records—state and federal
- Church Records—baptism, confirmation, membership, church history, etc.
- City Directories—businesses, residents, churches, etc.
- Court Records—divorce, criminal, guardianships, adoptions, name changes, etc.
- Fraternal Organizations—Masonic, Odd Fellows, Ancient Order of Hibernians, etc.
- Genealogical Societies—national, state, local, ethnic, etc.
- Historical Societies—local and state
- Immigration and Naturalization Records
- Land Records
- Libraries—local, county, regional, state, and college
- Lineage Organizations—Daughters/Sons of the American Revolution (DAR/SAR), Mayflower Society, etc.
- Military Records—service and pension files
- Newspapers
- Political Records—public and elected officials, political parties, etc.
- Probate or Estate Records
- Professional Organizations—American Medical Association, Bar Associations, Funeral Directors, etc.
- School Records—primary and secondary education
- Tax Records—property tax, head or poll tax lists, etc.
- Vital Records—births, marriages, and deaths
- Voter Registration Records

more than one state or area but it can be, and is, done every day by other researchers. Knowledge is the key to success.

There's an almost endless supply of sources that today's family historian can use to find additional information on an ancestor. Think creatively and make a list of all the places that your name appears on records, in newspapers, school records, yearbooks, etc., and then consider those sources as well. *The Genealogist's Companion & Sourcebook* by Emily Anne Croom is an excellent resource for both the beginner and the seasoned researcher. Croom provides an in-depth look at public sources in the United States and provides case studies as well as tips to show you how to make the most of these record types. You are sure to find sources you hadn't considered and some you didn't even know existed.

Whatever additional records you'll be using to further your research, be sure that you understand the following:

- Who created the original record?
- What will the record include or not include?
- When was it recorded?
- Where are the records stored?
- Why was the record created?
- How was the record compiled or constructed?

Always keep in mind my motto: "Research the record before you use the record for research!" Knowing the who, what, when, where, why, and how of every source will make you a more efficient researcher.

## RECORDS CHECKLIST

- Books—Bibles, diaries, letters, cards, journals, account books, baby books, scrapbooks, biographies, etc.

- Cemetery Records—names and locations of cemeteries, records of interments, etc.

- Census (State)—state and territorial population censuses taken by state government

- Census (Federal)—enumerations for population, agriculture, industry, mortality, slave, veterans, etc.

- Certificates—birth, christening, baptismal, confirmation, ordination, advancement, graduation, marriage, divorce, and death.

- Church Records—Sacraments (Baptisms, marriages, Confirmation, First Communion, etc.); Business (record purchases of pews, donations, etc.); Church history (member lists, Deacon's names, etc.)

- City Directories—lists of residents, businesses, churches, cemeteries, etc.

- County Histories—books or articles pertaining to the settlement and history of a given county

- Immigration and Naturalization Records—Naturalization certificates, Declarations of Intention, Petitions for Naturalization, repatriation certificates, etc.

- Land and Estate Records—deeds, mortgages, leases, wills, trust documents, tax records, homestead papers, bounty land warrants, proprietor's records, etc.

- Military Records—enlistment or induction notices, rosters, muster rolls, discharges, citations, pension records, state or local militia, World War I and II draft registration, Civil War, Revolutionary War, War of 1812, etc.

- Misc. Records—letters, pictures, naturalization, passports, school/university records, lodge, club and fraternity, business and insurance records, receipts and accounts.

- Newspapers—clippings from births, christenings, announcements, engagements, marriages, divorces, awards, deaths, obituaries, memorials, property transfers, etc.

- Passenger Lists—ship manifests of immigrants

- Pension Records—pensions for military service

- School Records—yearbooks, class lists, teacher, and staff lists, etc.

- Tombstone Transcriptions—published transcriptions of tombstones within a given cemetery or area

- Town Government Records—town meeting records, appointment of town officials, town reports listing town's budget and votes

- Vital Records—births, marriages, or deaths (town, county, and state compilations)

- Voter Records—lists of registered voters within the town

- Wills, Estates (Probate)—wills, estate inventories, court records pertaining to settlement of a deceased's estate and property

# NINE

# Reviewing Resources

N ow that you have laid the groundwork for all future research, you are ready to review what you have, decide what you need, and figure out how to achieve your goal—recording your family history. Regardless of how carefully you did your research in the first place, there is always additional information that you have not explored contained within your records. This is not a reflection on your research skills, but a fact that every family historian must acknowledge. As you progress in your research, you learn about additional family members, facts about your ancestors, and surnames that were unknown to you earlier in the process.

Whenever you solve a problem, such as determining an individual's parentage, you are presented with two more people to research. **Family history is ongoing, and you will find that there is truly no end to the possibilities for research and learning.**

## REVIEWING WHAT YOU'VE GATHERED

Periodically during your research you should review what you know. Creating a timeline for your ancestor or the family group is a good way to see where you might have blanks or holes in your information. Since family historians and genealogists work from the present and go backwards, it is easy to overlook portions of an ancestor's life. We might have a death, marriage, and birth record for the ancestor, but may not have compiled information about their education, occupations, etc. I once attended a lecture entitled "Investigating the Dash." At first the title intrigued me and now it has become my motto. The premise of the lecture was that a tombstone inscription reads "1813–1853," but what about the dash? What about the deceased's lifetime? His family, work, hobbies, hardships, etc. are represented by just a dash. A person deserves to be remembered for more than their birth and death dates. That is our job as family historians—to document what we can about their daily lives and record it for future generations.

A good exercise is to review all of the data you have accumulated on a single person or family group. If you have not yet created a list of what you learned about them, now is the time. I start with a page listing the birth and death dates of the individual broken down into decades. I list these dates on the left side of the page, leaving about ten lines blank after each date. This gives me a place to document each year of the given decade. You can also do this exercise on the computer and just insert the data wherever it fits chronologically without a problem. You are creating a timeline for the research subject.

Now that you have the format set up, you can systematically go through all of the records you have accumulated that are pertinent to the subject. When you look at the records you obtained many months or years ago, you will be looking at them with a fresh eye. Names that were unknown to you when you obtained the record should now be familiar. This is especially true of census records. Look at the neighborhood on the copy of the census page (remember what I said about photocopying it rather than just extracting the information?). Are there any other relatives whom you are now aware of living nearby? Did you look at every column on each and every census page you have? Did you follow through on all of the clues that were presented in other record sources? In the excitement of finding a census page, we may have overlooked some clues.

Now is the time to use these clues to locate additional records. If you missed a clue that the person owned property, you can now look for those records using the census dates as your guide to the years you should look at in the indexes. If the census record indicates that they did not own property in 1870 but they do in 1900, you should concentrate on the years 1870–1900. Where did they live when the 1880 census was taken (this census does not indicate home or land ownership)? You should begin looking at the deed indexes in the place of residence in 1870 and then in every place you know they resided through the 1900 census date. Watch the places of birth for any children to see if they moved around perhaps even to different states.

This is also a good time to go back to the original census films and look at previous or subsequent pages to the one you have. Since you have the entire citation, including the microfilm series, roll number, page number, etc., this should be an easy task. This review will also give you an opportunity to correct any incomplete citations.

Apply the same review tactics to every record you have. Take a look at the vital records or certificates that you acquired. Who are the witnesses? Are those names now familiar to you as belonging to or associated with the family? If not, why are they the witnesses to this particular document? How do they relate to the individual to whom the certificate or record pertains? Sometimes the answer to this lies in documents not even related to your family.

**Let's look at an example.** While transcribing the data from a birth recorded in Italy, I made note of the witnesses to the document. I tried to locate the names presented on the certificate within my family tree to no avail. While these two men (witnesses on Italian documents are almost always male) served as witnesses, I could find no connection to the family in question. When I looked back at the film containing the records, I looked at other records for that day and week. I found that these two men signed as witnesses on quite a few documents in addition to the ones for my family. Further research showed that the two men actually worked in the municipio (town hall) in the village. It seems that they acted as witnesses whenever they were needed.

If you have multiple census records and did not compile an overview form previously, this is the time to do so. In the process of transcribing the data from your copies to the overview form, you may be surprised to discover new facts or ones that conflict with what you know. Continue through the records in this manner until you have listed them on your timeline sheet. Are there gaps in certain decades? Have individuals or additional surnames appeared that need further research? Did you miss a particular census year? This is the time to make a list of possible research that you will need to do.

## TRANSCRIBING RECORDS

Additionally, you should make a full transcription of any land, probate, or other text documents that you've collected. Transcriptions are the best way to find hidden facts or clues within a text document. When you begin to transcribe them, you'll find some words that are unreadable or unfamiliar to you. When you encounter such a word or phrase, leave a blank in the typed version. You can always go back and fill it in later. The process of transcribing a document will include looking words up in dictionaries,

**Step By Step**

**For More Info**

**DICTIONARIES FOR GENEALOGISTS**

*A Medical Miscellany for Genealogists,* by Dr. Jeannette L. Jerger (Bowie, Md.: Heritage Books, Inc., 1995)

*Concise Genealogical Dictionary,* by Maureen and Glen Harris (Salt Lake City: Ancestry, Inc. 1989)

*What Did They Mean By That? A Dictionary of Historical Terms for Genealogists,* vol. 2, by Paul Drake, J.D. (Bowie, Md.: Heritage Books, Inc., 1998)

deciphering old handwriting, reading faded ink, and understanding variations in the spelling of words. If you are working with foreign records,
you add the element of translation as well.

When I make copies of documents, such as land records, I often make
copies of several additional records both before and after the one I need.
Since you will be using the copybooks, the same clerk will have written
most of the documents during a particular timeframe. Land records follow
a specific format and use almost exactly the same wording for each record
in that locale and time period. This practice can make it easier to make
out all the words or phrases on your record. Perhaps the word or phrase
is written more clearly in another record. I believe that anything that aids
you in your research is worth the price of a photocopy.

Keep in mind that your transcription should be a true and exact copy
of the original, to the best of your ability. All words and punctuation
should be recorded exactly as it is in the original document. Do not correct
spelling, punctuation, or capitalization errors. Your goal is to have an exact
typed copy of the original. I always begin the typed transcription with the
name of the document (e.g. land transfer, probate packet, etc.), to whom
the document pertains, and the complete citation of the record source.
When the transcription is complete, I print two copies. One copy can remain in your file with other documents, family group sheets, etc. The
second copy gets stapled to the original handwritten document. By doing
this, you'll always have a readable copy (who wants to try and read that
old chicken scratch again?) attached to the original along with the complete
citation. If and when the day comes that you share your research with
others, they'll be forever grateful for the typed version!

Following up on additional resources, looking at the original versions
of a document, and making sure you have missed nothing is crucial to
your research. I'm always reminded of this when I find a piece of data that
I missed early in my research years. Many times an answer might be right
there in the document, but I either didn't see it or didn't examine the
document carefully enough the first time. This is why review is so important. You will be a more skilled researcher and tuned in to the family after
you've spent considerable time researching them. Dissecting a document
and squeezing every bit of information from it will eventually become
second nature to you. Once you have read the record, ask yourself what
else is it telling you, perhaps in an indirect way?

**Tip**

Use *Reading Early American
Handwriting* by Kip Sperry
to practice your transcribing skills. He provides a
copy of the original document on one page and a
transcribed version on the
facing page. He also pro-
vides chapters on the styles
of handwriting, sample al-
phabets, abbreviations,
and some examples of ter-
minology that you might
encounter.

## START A RESEARCH TO-DO LIST

When you review previous research and make a list of the documents you've acquired, you may realize that you've missed some resources. Check your list of records against a checklist (see "Records Checklist" on pages 118-119) or against another family's records. Were there records that you used for one family that you forgot to find for another one? Some record types will show up in every family you research. Census records and birth, marriage, and death records are examples of these common sources. Making sure that you didn't miss any of these basic resources is important. If you neglected to get just one census record for a family, you might have missed a crucial piece of information and not have the data you need to locate additional records. Remember that every document you obtain should produce additional resources. If you don't find additional clues, you're not utilizing the information sufficiently.

Even a common record, such as a death certificate, can keep your research going for quite some time. Let's look at the clues or facts found in a twentieth-century death record.

Does the death record list

- a place of burial? Look for the cemetery records.
- an undertaker or funeral home name? Look for funeral home records.
- an address for the deceased? Check city directories to see who else might have lived at that address.
- an informant on the record? How is the informant related to the deceased?
- a cause of death? Was the death of a suspicious nature? Perhaps there is a coroner's inquest file or a medical examiner's report from the investigation.
- if the death a result of an accident? Was there a news account of it in the local papers?
- if the deceased was a veteran? Look for military service records.
- the names of the deceased's parents? Look for them in the census and other records.
- the place of birth for the deceased? Look for a birth record.
- the name of the deceased's spouse if they were married? Look for marriage records.

Was there an obituary or death notice published? If so, there may be a church mentioned where the deceased was a member, or the name of the clergyman officiating at the funeral may be given. The obituary or death notice might also list an undertaker's name, the cemetery of burial, and sometimes the names and residences of surviving family members. Some obituaries or death notices may even provide the place of birth for the parents of the deceased.

I came across a death record for a man that listed his cause of death as "drowning." His death occurred on Thanksgiving Day in 1900. The death wasn't listed as accidental and no further information was provided. I checked the newspapers for the week of the death looking for a news story, obituary, or a death notice with no luck. I even checked the newspaper for the local weather to see if it was warm enough for him to have been fishing, or cold enough to have been skating perhaps. It was too cold for fishing but too warm for skating or ice fishing, so the mystery continued.

The man was an immigrant from Nova Scotia who had a wife and several small children. It seemed that this tragedy would be something that would have made the papers in the small town in which they resided. My curiosity was piqued and I continued to look for clues. While talking to another researcher about the death, she suggested that I check the coroner's inquest records for the town to see if any investigation of the death was conducted. After determining where these records were, I looked up the date of his death. Sure enough, there it was! He had indeed drowned in the Charles River but the investigation showed that he'd come home, apparently drunk, and fallen face first into the river and drowned. No wonder the accident wasn't reported in the local paper. The family must have had a quiet funeral and burial to avoid embarrassment. If something about a record doesn't seem right, be sure to follow up on it.

While you are reviewing the documents you've accumulated, look carefully at every morsel of information—no matter how mundane it might seem. Look at the record from another perspective. **Compare it to other records for the same time period and place to see what is normally included.** What, if anything, is missing from your record? Are there lines or blanks that aren't filled in? Are records that should have been generated missing (e.g. a death notice or obituary, news item, etc.)? Ask yourself why these records are missing or nonexistent. Again, this is where knowing what *should* be included in a record is important. Sometimes I give the document to another researcher and have them tell me what additional records they would look at. A fresh eye might see something that you missed or think of a resource that you never considered.

Tip

## ETHNIC HERITAGE

While every family history is unique, there will always be common experiences, records, and documents from one family to another. If your family heritage is based on a foreign culture, you'll want to research the customs of that culture as well as the documents your ancestors generated. Ethnic heritage includes customs from the old country, certain religious practices and beliefs, migration and naming patterns, and perhaps artifacts that have been handed down in the family.

Besides reviewing the accumulated data for your family, you should learn something about the country and culture of your immigrant ancestors. How did their ethnic heritage dictate what types of jobs they held, what church they attended, their educational level, or whom they married? All of these questions should be asked, and hopefully answered, if you want to get a complete picture of their lives.

Genealogy and family history research are often difficult pursuits. You'll hit many roadblocks and brick walls in your research. You'll experience frustration and excitement, tragedy and triumph, and at times you will be totally amazed by what you discover. If you want a hobby that is easy—this is not the right hobby! However, you'll be hard-pressed to find a hobby that is as rewarding and revealing as the search for *your* family's history. When you've thoroughly "investigated the dash" and know your ancestors almost as well as you know yourself, then—and only then—will you understand the rewards of this adventure. You will know your ancestors as human beings with their own dreams and goals, hardships and joys, and truly appreciate how their lives have helped to determined yours. It's a wonderful journey!

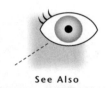

**See Also**

Read *A Genealogist's Guide to Discovering Your Immigrant & Ethnic Ancestors* by Sharon DeBartolo Carmack for more information on ethnic research.

**TEN**

# Sharing Data

R esearching your family history is a time-consuming but rewarding pursuit. Many hours have gone into compiling and documenting that research, and it is important to share your data with family and fellow researchers, especially on the Internet. Doing so in a responsible manner will assure that your research is available to future generations and may also help you to make contact with others researching the same families.

**From the very beginning of your research, you should be documenting and citing your sources.** Many researchers have trouble understanding what the source citation should include. When the information you're presenting comes from a Web site, it's important to cite the Web site address, the title of the Web site, the author, and the date that you found the information on that site. The same rules apply to recording information that came from an e-mail. List the person's name, e-mail address, and date of the e-mail. Due to the fleeting nature of Internet sites, e-mail addresses, and URLs, you may not be able to find the information again at a later date.

If the information you are adding to your pedigree was obtained from a published source (a newspaper, book, periodical, etc.), you'll need to list the title, author, publication date, and page number. I also like to add the library or facility where I found the source material. Some books and resources are scarce and hard to find. I have found that I may need to go back to the book or original source to check something years later. Knowing which of the hundreds of libraries and research facilities I found it in is a real time-saver. This is especially helpful if you are using a microfilm copy of the records.

**Citing Sources**

See *Evidence!: Citation & Analysis for the Family Historian,* by Elizabeth Shown Mills.

Let's say you find a marriage record on a roll of microfilm. It will be a picture of the original paper record, which is stored in a repository somewhere. Perhaps these records no longer exist except in the microfilmed format. Other researchers will need to know that you did not see the original paper record but only a photo or film copy of it. This will save them many hours of fruitless searching for the originals. List the film number, publisher, filming date, and where you found the microfilm. If the film is from the Family History Library in Salt Lake City, the film will probably be available to view at any local FHC (Family History Center). Having the film number makes ordering the roll of microfilm an easy job.

Many beginners make the mistake of citing or recording incorrect information. When they cite a source for a marriage date, for example, they often list "marriage license" or "family Bible" as the source. The license and family Bible are the records, not the sources. Who had possession of the record when you saw it? Where was the original located? When you list or cite a source, include the information that will enable any researcher to go right to the book, microfilm, periodical, courthouse, etc. where you got your information. If the record is an original copy of a family record that you or a relative have in your possession, you should include the name of the person who has possession of the document, their relationship to the marriage participants, and when the record was viewed.

## WHERE DID IT COME FROM?

A bibliography on a Web site or in a book usually tells the reader all of the books and sources used in the research. Having such a bibliography is better than nothing, but trying to determine which facts came from which sources can be a tedious task. Similar to many of the CD-ROMs and databases available that combine several books or sources into one database, you're left to figure out what facts came from where. If you've ever found such information, you know how frustrating this can be.

When a birth, marriage, or death is listed, the seasoned researcher knows that there may be incorrect data included. Did you look at the original document or a county or state copy? What civil or religious body created the first record of the event? You must know which is the primary record of any event. There may be later copies sent to the state or other governing bodies. These may be photocopies, but are more often hand-transcribed from the original. Was all of the data transcribed? Was it copied correctly? Was information deleted from the original? Does the information agree with other

**Tip**

**HELPFUL HINT**

Whenever you have an opportunity to look at original records, it is always wise to get a photocopy or picture of it to help to ensure future generations will be able to see it. With today's technology, scanning or photographing records and photos is a relatively easy process.

records you have? If the data conflicts with information other researchers have gathered personally, you should look for further evidence to determine which fact is correct. Do the dates, names, and places make sense in the overall picture or timeline of the individual's life? Ask the same questions whether you found the information or another researcher provided it.

**A good researcher will always be a bit skeptical of any facts presented, whether there is documentation or not.** Just because an author lists sources it doesn't mean that she copied or interpreted the data accurately. Did she read the handwritten document correctly? Does the record actually exist or did she make it up? Did she make a leap of faith that the Joseph Rogers listed in the cited document is the correct Joseph Rogers? Pedigrees, just like records, must have continuity to them. One record cannot, and does not, stand on its own. Each fact needs to be supported with additional evidence.

Important

When using published books, check for source material. Even if the research is heavily sourced, you should check some of the references to determine how carefully the author used those sources. I've found some source citations that included volume and page numbers for records that I was unable to locate, or where the volume and page cited was a totally different document. Where the author found them is still a mystery. It's always smart to check out some of the citations in any book or on a Web site to determine their reliability.

When you find an author whose citations are complete, accurate, and always where he states they are, you have found one of the rare jewels of the genealogical world! I have not found too many of these. An amazing example of a well-documented genealogy is *The John Round Family of Swansea and Rehoboth, Massachusetts* by H.C. Peter Rounds (Baltimore: Gateway Press, 1983). His book is probably the best documented book I've ever seen. He presents more than eight pages of sources and provides the reader with exact citations. I've never found a single citation in this book to be inaccurate. Thankfully it's also my maternal grandmother's family line. How lucky could I be?

Whenever you cite a source you must ask yourself, "Can I duplicate this research using only the information in my citation?" This is the quickest way to determine if your citations are complete. Here's an example: After using several census indexes, both online and on CD-ROM, I located Patrick Shea in the 1910 federal census. I printed the page, then I entered the data on a family group sheet and in my database, and cited my source.

Some researcher might cite the source as the 1910 census for Massachusetts. This is a terribly incomplete citation. Is it referring to the federal census or a state census? What town or county was Patrick in? A complete and correct citation would include the:

- Author—NARA (National Archives and Records Administration)
- Year—1910
- Type of record—federal census
- Microfilm series number—T624
- Microfilm roll number—#617
- State—Massachusetts
- County—Suffolk
- Town/city—Boston
- Enumeration district—#1386
- Page number—#43

By listing all of the above information, I've ensured that any researcher could walk into a NARA facility and go right to the cabinet housing the 1910 federal census microfilms. Then they could verify the series number, get the correct roll of film, and go directly to the record that I've used without reindexing or looking anything up. That makes for a great citation! Can you do that with your source citations? There are some software programs (the one I use is called *Clooz* by Ancestor Detective <www.clooz.com>) that offer citation templates, depending on the record used. Such software is a wonderful tool for practicing how to format the information and for knowing that you've included all of the pertinent details in the citation. Using the source templates in your genealogy program or in software like *Clooz* will prompt you to include all of the information. Check your genealogy software to see how it handles source citations. Another program, RootsMagic <www.rootsmagic.com>, prompts me to include all of the details and even provides source wizards for a variety of record types. The source wizards are formatted to assure that all pertinent information is included.

## PUBLISHING AND SHARING

Many researchers hesitate to publish or share their research until they feel it is completed. Unfortunately, no family history is ever complete. Every individual you add to your tree also adds two parents, perhaps siblings, and many additional questions. Genealogy is the only hobby that gets more difficult as you become more experienced. The further back you get the more difficult it is to prove even basic facts. So when will you consider it

**For More Info**

**COMPUTER BOOKS**

*Online Roots,* by Pamela Boyer Porter and Amy Johnson Crow (Nashville, Tenn.: Rutledge Hill Press, 2003)

*Planting Your Family Tree Online,* by Cyndi Howells (Nashville, Tenn.: Rutledge Hill Press, 2003)

*The Genealogist's Computer Companion,* by Rhonda R. McClure (Cincinnati: Betterway Books, 2002)

complete and worthy of sharing? Since many of us begin this type of project when we are older, perhaps retired, it's all the more important that we share it with others often.

**This sharing can be as simple as providing copies of the current research to cousins, siblings, or others interested in your research.** Printing out a copy and simply distributing it, perhaps every year, is a good idea. None of us like to face the fact that we will not always be around, but it's a fact of life. If something happened to you tomorrow, would anyone know what research you've already done? You can always update, correct, or otherwise add to your information at any time. You should, however, keep track of when and where the copies were distributed.

Reminder

Some of the locations that are crucial to other researchers may not be obvious to many of us. Whenever you distribute data, think about the places that the individuals you're researching lived. If you were looking for information on a specific person or family, where would you look? These are the places where you need to deposit copies of your research. These might include local libraries, historical or genealogical societies, state or county libraries, or other organizations, along with other relatives. Many local historical and genealogical societies have files that people have donated with compiled research. These files may go back fifty or more years and may contain a copy of an original family Bible, documents, or other artifacts.

Nearly eight years ago, I sent a copy of some research I was doing for a friend to a genealogical and historical society in Illinois—the state the family was from. I included what I knew, mostly from family papers and a family Bible, and asked if anyone had any additional information. As always, I included all of my contact information, just in case. About a year ago, I got a package in the mail from another researcher in Illinois. She'd gone to the county historical and genealogical society library to do some research and came across my file. The society had filed it under the surname in question. She was a descendant of the sister of my research subject, who was an adopted child. Not only did she have additional information on the family and siblings, but she had the information regarding his birth parents! She sent me all of this information and included many photographs of the man and his family. She told the story of his adoption and what events caused him to become an orphan. Amazing! Because my e-mail address had changed she was unable to contact me via the Internet, so she sent the package to my mailing address, which thankfully had not changed. You just never know when or where information will come to you.

Whenever you visit local, county, or state societies or libraries, ask if they have such a repository for family papers and research. If so, ask them in what format they would like the data. Some like it in a binder, while others will accept loose papers in a file folder. I prefer to put the data in a report cover or a binder, depending on the amount of paper involved. You should always be sure to include your contact information should another researcher want to ask about the research or perhaps share additional data with you.

Keep a list of all of the locations and people that have copies, as you'll want to know where to update your contact information or share future discoveries. This is especially true for data posted on the Internet. Nothing is more frustrating than to find information on your family that another researcher has posted and not be able to contact them. One student recently offered a great tip in one of my classes. She suggested using an e-mail address from one of the national companies that offer free e-mail accounts (Hotmail, Yahoo, etc.) for all genealogical postings. That way, no matter how many times she changed her Internet provider or her e-mail address, the free service address would remain the same. It also helped her keep genealogical correspondence out of her everyday e-mail box. Something to consider.

## DISTRIBUTING COPIES

Many years ago I transcribed a book of poetry written by my great-grandmother, Teresa (Emery) Rogers. I printed copies from my computer files and distributed them to my cousins, all of whom shared this great-grandmother. That means that twelve copies are in the hands of Teresa's descendants. Copies were also given to her grandchildren, including my mother, for a total of twenty copies. Copies were also printed and deposited in the historical society located in each town Teresa resided in during her life. An additional copy went to the state genealogical society library in each state of residency. Today nearly thirty-five copies of this transcription are distributed from Vermont to Michigan. The same applies to the pedigree charts and other data relating to her life and the lives of her ancestors and descendants (excluding those individuals still living).

Family research that includes pedigree and family group sheets along with copies of documents, photos, etc., can be distributed in the same way. **I've found over the years that when I share the family research, stories, and photographs with others, I almost always receive additional information, stories, and photos from relatives.** This has resulted in many new finds. Sharing

Tip

data, photos, and other items of common interest opens the lines of communication. Perhaps one of the cousins has the original family Bible and is willing to make copies so that the information may be shared.

I have published certain family lines in other publications when the opportunity arises. The *Vermont Families in 1791* series, edited by Scott Andrew Bartley (Pittsford, Vt.: Genealogical Society of Vermont, 1997), contains the ancestry of Teresa's husband, Hoxey Constant Rogers, in volume two. My contact information is included and I have received additional information as a result of the effort. Many of the researchers who submitted pedigrees to this publication have aided other researchers over the years. Many societies print family lineages in their regular or yearly publications to aid others researching the same lines. Placing your data in localities where others would think to look for it is an important step.

Another important benefit of distributing your research on a regular basis is preservation. If you keep all of the data on your computer or on paper, hoping to publish it "someday," what happens if there is a fire, computer crash, or other disaster (including your own death) before you do so? Will all of the research and data be lost? Distributing what you have on a regular basis, as well as keeping a print copy away from the original, will help assure the survival of your work. If you know of another family member who's interested in your research, be sure to let others know (perhaps in your will) that your research papers should be given to them or to a specified society or organization. Will others know what all the papers and files are about? Will they understand their importance? Do not leave the survival of your life's work to chance.

## ON THE INTERNET

With today's technology we have the ability to share our research with thousands of individuals with little effort. Whether you construct a family Web site of your own or share your research on one of the many sites that allow you to post family trees, you have a responsibility to be sure that your research is as accurate as possible. Look for ways to share the data that allows you to keep your sources and notes with the facts. Many Web sites don't have the capability of maintaining the sources when the tree is posted. Facts without proof are fiction!

In addition, be cautious about sharing data on living individuals. With identity theft a hot topic in the twenty-first century, we must be sensitive to the possibility that someone might use this information for illegal purposes.

Listing a person's name, birth date, and place of birth might enable someone else to obtain a copy of that birth certificate or other identification to
be used for illegal purposes.

We must also be careful with the sensitive information we might possess.
Illegitimate births, divorces, and other family skeletons shouldn't be posted
in a public forum. We must be sensitive to other relatives' concerns regarding family facts and stories. While you might include some of these facts
or stories in copies of your research given to relatives, they should *never*
be posted on the Internet. As mentioned in the chapter on oral histories,
we must honor our promises to others regarding sensitive information. If
you stated that the data would not be shared, then DO NOT share it!

Genealogists as a group tend to be helpful and willing to share information readily. It's hard for us to understand that not all individuals are
honest and want the information for research purposes only. Being a bit
of a skeptic goes a long way in protecting the rights of living individuals.
Ask yourself if you would want your information posted on the Web for
all to see. There is enough personal information out there in cyberspace
on each and every one of us—why add to it?

## Ways to Post Data on the Internet

While there are a myriad of sites willing to allow you to upload your family
research, you must read the fine print. When you upload your data, does it
become the property of the web site owners? Can they publish the data and
sell it? Who has access to it? Is it included in a paid subscription database
or free to anyone who wishes to see it? These are important questions to
ask. **Read the rules and regulations before you accept them or post information.**
Some Web sites will give you free Web space to upload your genealogical
research. By accepting the free Web space, you may in effect be giving them
permission to publish your data without further consent from you.

**Important**

Some Web sites that accept genealogical research will "clean" the data
(remove information on anyone still living), while others never look at the
information posted. If a person's data lists a birth date less than one hundred
years ago but does not include a death date, that person should be considered
living and the data should be removed from the file before it's uploaded.
Even if you know that the person is deceased, you must be careful of the
data for recent generations. For example, my bank asked me for my mother's
maiden name as a password to access information on my accounts. Genealogists who post this information risk having it used for illegal purposes.

## Mail Lists and Web Postings

While you may not be ready to publish your research in its entirety, you can post portions of the research in a lot of different places. Whenever you're researching in a specific geographic area, you'll want to see what sites might exist. You can post queries or information you might have, especially if you have some original documents pertaining to the family. More and more researchers are digitizing photographs and documents so they may be shared.

Nearly eight years ago I worked on a family project for a friend of mine. Being unfamiliar with researching in Wisconsin and Illinois, I needed the assistance of people living in that geographic area. Using USGenWeb <www.usgenweb.org>, I learned about the area, what records were available, what societies were in the area, relevant publications, and historic details. The Wisconsin GenWeb state page had links to the county pages for the three counties I was interested in. After spending some time checking the county pages to see what might be there, I decided to sign up for the e-mail lists specific to those counties. E-mail lists are a place that researchers can ask questions, post information, and otherwise correspond with like-minded researchers.

When you sign up for an e-mail list, there are usually two options available. The first is a straight mail list. This option allows you to receive (in your inbox) a copy of each posting to the list as an individual e-mail. In this mode, where each message is sent separately, you can easily save any message that you wish and delete those that aren't of interest. You will, however, get many messages each day, depending on the popularity of that list. The second option is the digest mode. The digest mode compiles all of the messages posted on a given day and forwards them to the subscribers as one e-mail. There are pros and cons to both options. In the digest mode, you'll only get one message each day and not have dozens of individual messages lined up in your inbox. The drawback to the digest mode is that you must copy messages you wish to save to another file before you delete the digest of that day's postings. The nice thing about most e-mail lists is that you can try out one option and change it later, if needed.

Regardless, when you sign up for e-mail lists (most are part of the Roots-Web site <www.rootsweb.com> or the USGenWeb <www.usgenweb.org>), you should save the instructions on how to unsubscribe from the list. Almost every list I subscribe to will send you an e-mail confirming your request to subscribe. This e-mail will contain information on acceptable posts, canceling your subscription, and other rules specific to that list. I print these out and keep them together in a binder. You can categorize them by locality, surname, or other subject matter. Saving the e-mail in a place where you can find it makes unsubscribing much easier. It's a good idea to unsubscribe if you are going to be away from your computer for extended periods. Nothing is worse than coming home from a two-week vacation to find hundreds of e-mails that you'll have to wade through in your inbox. This is another advantage of the digest mode, since there will be only one message for each day you are gone.

Most e-mail lists also archive the messages they receive. In many cases you can search the archive for messages that were posted before you subscribed. Some of these archives go back years. Who knows, you may just find cousins you didn't know about!

## COPYRIGHT ISSUES

Whenever you publish any data, either online or in print format, you must be aware of copyright laws. Posting transcriptions or text from published books often constitutes copyright infringement. Many family history researchers think that by posting information from books they are helping other researchers. While the data may be helpful, you are violating the author's copyright and depriving him or her of the royalties earned for all of their hard work. If you wish to include portions of copyrighted material you must get written permission from the author to do so. **You must also be sure to properly credit the original author of the material.** Copyright laws and restrictions also apply to photographs, especially those taken by professional photographers or studios.

**Citing Sources**

Occasionally a researcher will obtain data from another researcher, a Web site, pedigree file, or even a book that they will then incorporate into their database. Many times they accept the data as it's presented without verifying any of the facts. We all have some of this data in our pedigrees, especially from our early research before we knew better (yes, even I do!). Once it's incorporated into your files, you may inadvertently post it on a Web site or publish it elsewhere. You have now put your reputation on the line. What if the data were inaccurate or entirely false? The person seeing your posting might assume that your research can't be trusted. Publish only what you have proven to be fact. If you include assumptions, they should be well documented. Most current sites don't allow you to attach notes to specific data, so therein lies a dilemma. What should you share? If researchers were a little more cautious before posting data, there might not be so many mistakes and false pedigrees floating around in cyberspace.

When one person makes a mistake in his research and then posts that research on the Internet, others may inadvertently pass it along. Once posted in cyberspace, facts and lies travel at the same speed! The data that I shared with a cousin nearly fifteen years ago and subsequently determined to be incorrect is now published on a Family Tree Maker disk and sold to other researchers. My name (thankfully) appears nowhere on the file, but I know that the mistakes are all mine. She had no right to post research that she herself did not perform.

One of the greatest benefits of posting queries, information, or research interests on the Internet is the potential of networking with others with similar interests. By putting information out into cyberspace, you enable others to find you and share. Several years ago, I joined an Internet group that is interested in a specific area in Italy. My posting of some photographs from a town in Calabria netted me a second cousin whose parents still live there. He contacted me after seeing my photos. He asked why I was interested in his beloved hometown. When I explained that my grandfather was born there, he recognized the surname as that of his mother. One thing led to another, and we determined that his great-grandfather and my grandfather were the only two sons in that family. One settled in America and the other returned to Calabria to raise his family. Even better, his parents still live in the family home where my grandfather was born nearly 130 years ago. This cousin and I have shared pictures of the family on both sides of the Atlantic; he provided me with photos of the church where my grandfather was baptized; and I was able to share stories of his great-grandfather as related to me by my ninety-seven-year-old aunt, who knew her Uncle Frank personally! It doesn't get any better than that!

Now that we have covered the many aspects of creating your family history, recording it for future generations, and sharing that research, you may feel overwhelmed. Just take it one step at a time, conquer one stone wall at a time, and persevere—you will be so glad you did.

**Internet Source**

**WEB SITES FOR COPYRIGHT ISSUES**

U.S. Copyright Office <http://lcweb.loc.gov/copyright>

Cyndi's List <www.CyndisList.com/copyrite.htm>

U.S. Copyright and Genealogy site <http://stellar-one.com/copyrightgenealogy>

# Index